New Perspectives

America and the Origins
of the Cold War

Edited by
JAMES V. COMPTON
San Francisco State College

Houghton Mifflin Company • **Boston**
New York • *Atlanta* • *Geneva, Illinois* • *Dallas* • *Palo Alto*

Printed in the U.S.A.

Library of Congress Catalog Card Number: 71-169722

ISBN: 0-395-12080-2

26882

To Jamie and Nell Imbrie
who questioned the conventional wisdom
from the start

Contents

v

III   The Cold War in Perspective   127

History is lived forwards but is written in retrospect. We know the end before we consider the beginning and we can never wholly recapture what it was to know the beginning only.

C. V. Wedgewood

Introduction

A vast historical literature inevitably comes to surround the wars men have fought. The drama of battle, the inquiry into causes and results, the endless debate over blame and inevitability, all have a natural fascination for professional and amateur historians. It is rather more remarkable that a literature of massive proportions should have been produced about a war which never quite happened—a unique, yet understandable phenomenon of modern historiography. The cold war is obviously high historical drama: thrusts and counterthrusts on the diplomatic chessboard, salvationist rhetoric and crusading zeal in the world forums, soured hopes and morbid anxieties in the minds of millions, evocation of universalist devils and transcendent moral principles in the national capitals, massive deployment of military power by the two protagonists up to, but never quite over, the line of armed conflict. Adding to the tension is the disquieting knowledge that a translation from cold to hot war with nuclear capabilities could threaten human survival.

A glance at the selected bibliography at the end of this book should persuade the reader that this curious episode we call the cold war has indeed been the subject of a wide-ranging and intensive analysis. It is equally clear, however, that as yet no satisfactory consensus on the origin and nature of the war has come out of this welter of material. In fact, disagreement over these questions appears to grow increasingly broader and more complex as schools of thought divide and subdivide. The debate itself, however, is highly significant, for it has raised important fundamental issues transcending the cold war, even though a final historical perspective continues to elude us.

This book aims at providing the reader interested in modern history an introduction to one aspect of the cold war—the question of its origins, with particular emphasis on the American influence. The study is confined to Europe and America in the years 1943 to 1947, since it was the collapse of the World War II alliance and the actions and reactions of the United States and the Soviet Union over the prostrate body of Europe which precipitated the first frosty outlines of a conflict destined to dominate the international scene in the mid-twentieth century.

Who was to blame for the cold war? Who started it? Which of the two major powers will have to bear the greater burden of historical guilt? The quest for villainy is always an intriguing one and, when pursued with decent respect for historical perspective, is perfectly legitimate. Ultimately, however, this question may be secondary to another problem, namely: What exactly was the cold war? This quest for meaning becomes especially complex because of the dual nature of the conflict. At the end of the war, there emerged certain quite circumscribed points of geopolitical conflict between the United States and the Soviet Union, more or less definable in time and space, and running for the most part along a line "from Stettin to Trieste"—a line which was to become the "iron curtain" in Winston Churchill's famous words.

The concrete points of tension were certainly formidable enough in themselves: economic reconstruction in the U.S.S.R. and in Europe, disarmament and international control of atomic weaponry, Soviet strategic sensitivities in Eastern Europe and the liberal guarantees of the Atlantic Charter, the Polish question, the German question; to name some of the salient frictions. In addition, the resurgence of the maimed feelings and suppressed suspicions implicit in the wartime alliance, the yawning gulf between economic, political, and ideological perspectives, the gross disequilibrium of power, to say nothing of the myriad of often conflicting domestic pressures within both countries, made the atmosphere at the end of the war not altogether conducive to an easy resolution of the issues between the two superpowers.

Yet, under different historical circumstances, these questions, while certainly productive of much tension and hostility, might well have been kept within manageable limits and handled through normal diplomatic processes. However, it was clear by 1947 (and stirrings were evident earlier) that the cold war was to move beyond normal international relations to a more exalted level. The rhetoric on both sides rose above actual points of conflict into the realm of global crusading, with each side assuring the unconverted and unanointed that earthly salvation lay exclusively in the voluntary or enforced acceptance of their particular form of political and economic organization. In this increasingly Manichaean perspective, those who dallied with neutralism or trafficked with "them" faced the moral, political, and perhaps nuclear wrath of the other side. This absolutist "we-they" syndrome—this mythic aspect of the cold war—was replete with self-fulfilling prophecies and not without elements of psychic gratification to both sides.

How did this bizarre situation come about? Some commentators have stressed the postwar emergence of new forums, audiences, and instruments of propaganda, which almost begged for exploitation. Others find the answer in a similar characteristic of both American and Russian political culture, namely, a national messiah complex, exhibited in the earliest traditions of the two powers and fostered by an ironic parallelism in historical development, the earlier formulations simply adapted to twentieth-century requirements. Accordingly, the "third Rome" of old Muscovy became the "socialist motherland," and the "refuge for mankind" of old Philadelphia became "the arsenal of democracy."

In any event, the evolution of the cold war as a two-tiered conflict, revealing both an operational (geopolitical) and a nominal (rhetorical) level, profoundly obscured the central problem considered in this book, the nature and origins of the war. The rhetoric itself became a substantial factor rendering nonnegotiable otherwise negotiable issues; closing options; compelling exaggerated postures, intemperate abuse, and imputation of direst motives; and generally distorting the usual processes of international adjustment. This moral inflation was fully in gear by 1947 reaching a climax in the early 1950s, as reflected domestically by the embodiment of cold war anxieties in the person of Senator Joseph McCarthy. Yet, at the same time on the operational level, the two powers were compelled to face a de facto stand-off, and the European cold war in its classic, bipolar form was, in fact, subsiding. Thus, historians have faced a formidable task in trying to untangle the origins of this complex and frightening world situation which evolved after World War II, and some of the writings reveal certain of the nominal-operational confusions characteristic of the war itself.

At the end of every war, a body of historical literature appears, aimed at revising the generally accepted view of the origin of the conflict and at reapportioning the blame for what has happened among the contestants. The cold war has been no exception. In fact, there have been two waves of revisionist assault on the orthodox view that the cold war was foisted on an innocent America by an aggressive Russia. Just after the war a number of books and articles appeared attributing the unfortunate world situation more or less exclusively to the stupidity or treachery of the Roosevelt administration, which had, it was argued, sold Eastern Europe (and much more, as well) down the river to the Soviets. These writers often depicted a relatively continuous and subversive conspiracy to sell out to the Soviets from 1933 on, the fear of which was not to be entirely expunged from American life even under the Truman and Eisenhower administrations.

The second wave, both quantitatively and qualitatively more substantial, flourished in the 1960s with some precursors in the 1950s and took precisely the opposite tack, as will be seen in the readings. History, of course, is not written in a vacuum; thus, it is not surprising that the first attack, from the right, appeared during a period of domestic reaction against Communism, while the second wave, from the left, appeared at a time of mounting disillusionment with cold war policies, especially as applied in Indochina. Since historiographic dispute so often reflects and effects the intellectual and political history of the time in which it is written, the problem of partison bias and present-mindedness can become acute.

The orthodox and revisionist cases will be explored more fully in the readings which follow. In brief, orthodox historians see the cold war as an American response (essentially legitimate, although sometimes maladroit) to an objective condition in postwar international affairs)—the expansionist tendencies in Soviet foreign policy which threatened the survival of liberal institutions and of American security interests in Europe. The revisionists, on the other hand, view the situation as an American provocation of the U.S.S.R. caused either by a gross misreading of Soviet policy or an insensitivity to legitimate Soviet anxieties and security interests. They also consider more specific economic and political needs of the United States to be a possible motivating factor. Mention should perhaps be made of a third strain of thought which, somewhat less interested in the guilt question, believes the conflict originated in the great forces of twentieth-century world history—forces which, in turn, were conditioned by the vastly differing historical experiences of the two powers—culminating in World War II, particularly in Soviet-American relations during that period.

The debate, then, is usually interpreted as a fairly straightforward argument between orthodox and revisionist commentators. However, like the cold war itself, the matter is more complex; at least two other questions cut across the basic argument. First is the problem of the motivation and of the essential character of American policy. Both orthodox and revisionist historians are divided among themselves on such questions as the alleged shift of policy in the transition from Roosevelt to Truman, the elements of naïveté and calculation, the factors of realism and idealism, and the respective significance of economic and nuclear influences. These disagreements over interpretation immediately raise the second question—the historical inevitability of the cold war. This problem has also caused division within both camps. Thus, in dealing with the subject of blame (touched upon by virtually all the writers), more fundamental questions relating to the nature of the conflict have inevitably been illuminated.

For the foreseeable future controversy will continue to swirl around the nature and origins of the cold war. A unifying synthesis, satisfactory to all schools of thought, is scarcely more imaginable regarding this episode than regarding, say, the American Civil War. One overriding consideration in cold war research and commentary insures the perpetuation of the argument; simply, unlike the material available on the Civil War, there is documentary evidence from only one side of the cold war. Abundant American archival and other material is available, but judgments of the validity of American policy are to some degree contingent upon estimations of Soviet intentions during those years. At this point, however, investigations must move from interpretation based on fact into conjecture, inference, and hypothesis. Until and unless Soviet archives are opened or Soviet officials show some inclination to collaborate with the Oral History Project (neither, it would appear, being altogether promising prospects), it simply cannot be said with any certainty just what the Soviets had in mind during those years, nor just what internal pressures and problems influenced their policy.

However, the student of the cold war should not despair entirely; from the morass of conflicting literature is emerging, if not a grand synthesis, then at least partial agreement on some aspects of the problem. Most writers agree, for example, that the nominal-rhetorical aspect of the cold war, while explainable in political-cultural terms, represented a deplorable and dangerous overreaction on both sides. Most authors agree about the specific areas of conflict: Eastern Europe, Germany, economic relations, and control of nuclear weapons. Most also concede that elements of innocent or calculated insensitivity and of misunderstanding characterized Soviet-American relations. There is a growing predilection among orthodox and revisionist commentators alike to modify Stalin's cold war image as a world revolutionary and to accept at least the possibility that the Soviet leader was a Russian nationalist motivated largely by considerations of national security and economic recovery. Finally, an increasing number of writers have offered the proposition that in three areas—guarantees against German rearmament and aggression, nonpolitical American economic assistance to Russia, and international nuclear control—the United States might well have used greater imagination and flexibility in exploring various options, without undue risk to American security interests. Such initiatives in the early years could not have prevented the cold war, but it has been suggested they might have made it more manageable and less dangerous. Building on these fairly limited points, the possibility exists that wider areas of agreement will gradually emerge as the investigation continues. For the moment, however, large areas of controversy remain and whatever enlightenment can be gained will have to come from the debate.

This small volume cannot, of course, provide a full chronological narrative of events. Rather the purpose is to focus on certain developments which all schools of thought agree are crucial to an understanding of the origins of the cold war and to an attempt to reach the core of the historiographic argument.

The first section consists of three fairly general readings which develop the orthodox framework including the differing emphases within the more conventional writing. The second part deals with revisionist criticism of certain more specific aspects of American policy: the bomb, economic relations, Eastern Europe, and the evolution of American cold war policy in practice (the Truman Doctrine) and theory (containment). The third part is more general, summarizing certain questions, presenting a panel discussion, and exploring the broader aspects of the historical debate transcending the cold war itself.

As the student wanders through the thickets of this complex problem, he should be especially on guard against the siren song of present-mindedness in its cruder forms. No one can resist it entirely; perfect objectivity, like perfect justice, remains a mirage. Still, the student of history has an obligation to try to approach this goal at least in his methodology. On the other hand, the historian is as much entitled to exercise moral judgment as anyone else, and his standards cannot help being affected to some degree by his perspectives on his own time. Further, his personal predispositions will influence his selection of subject and his conclusions. Perhaps some refuge from this problem (which is discussed in the final two articles of the book) can be found in an old conception of British law which holds that justice must not only be done but be *seen* to be done. So it is with historical judgment on men in high places and on their policies. In the context and circumstances of the time, as nearly as they can be reconstructed, given the momentum of ongoing movements and tendencies, and the immense pressures on fallible human beings, one must ask what courses of action, which options, were open, and *seen* to be open *then,* to the main actors in the early cold war drama.

It should also be remembered that statesmen and political leaders, assuming they are neither fools nor monsters, are constantly confronted with a dilemma. On the one hand, they are obliged, as defenders of the national interest, to plan for the worst eventuality in a given international situation. On the other hand, unless impasse and *immobilisme* are to become a way of life, they must also be prepared, from time to time, to take certain calculated risks in an effort to reach agreement and thereby avoid the higher dangers accompanying a prolonged period of frustration. The student may well want to ask himself whether American leaders, in the early years of the cold war, struck the most appropriate and productive balance between these two imperatives as was possible under the circumstances.

A discerning and open-minded investigation of the United States and the origins of the cold war cannot only help explain a singularly ominous event of modern history but can throw some light on broader questions as well: the role of objectivity and morality in historical judgment, the problem of historical inevitability, the dynamics of foreign policy formulation in our time, and the relationship of the immediate past to the present.

I   The Orthodox Framework

The three selections presenting the more conventional perspective illustrate how orthodox emphases vary considerably. Schlesinger, in his treatment of the wartime years, attempts to view developments as they may have appeared to the Soviets as well as to the Americans. He is also often critical of certain American attitudes and reactions, in keeping with the "realist" school which tends to deplore moralistic, legalistic, and universalist elements in American foreign policy. Spanier, on the other hand, in his discussion of the years 1946–1947, accepts more or less uncritically the traditional theory of cold war origins and development, finding the American response not only legitimate but also appropriate. Halle critically analyzes the role of myth and rhetoric in the cold war and stresses the virtual inevitability of what happened.

Nevertheless, all three agree that the cold war was *essentially* initiated by the Soviet Union forcing the United States to make a corrective response, and, therefore, the burden of blame must be assigned to the U. S. S. R.

ARTHUR M. SCHLESINGER, JR.
Origins of the Cold War

PEACEMAKING AFTER THE Second World War was not so much a tapestry as it was a hopelessly raveled and knotted mess of yarn. Yet, for purposes of clarity, it is essential to follow certain threads. One theme indispensable to an understanding of the Cold War is the contrast between two clashing views of world order: the "universalist" view, by which all nations shared a common interest in all the affairs of the world, and the "sphere-of-influence" view, by which each great power would be assured by the other great powers of an acknowledged predominance in its own area of special interest. The universalist view assumed that national security would be guaranteed by an international organization. The sphere-of-interest view assumed that national security would be guaranteed by the balance of power. While in practice these views have by no means been incompatible (indeed, our shaky peace has been based on a combination of the two), in the abstract they involved sharp contradictions.

The tradition of American thought in these matters was universalist—or Wilsonian. Roosevelt had been a member of Wilson's sub-cabinet, in 1920, as candidate for Vice President, he had campaigned for the League of Nations. It is true that, within Roosevelt's infinitely complex mind, Wilsonianism warred with the perception of vital strategic interests he had imbibed from Mahan. Moreover, his temperamental inclination to settle things with fellow princes around the conference table led him to regard the Big Three—or Four—as trustees for the rest of the world. On occasion, as this narrative will show, he was beguiled into flirtation with the sphere-of-influence heresy. But in principle he believed in joint action and remained a Wilsonian. His hope for Yalta, as he told the Congress on his return, was that it would "spell the end of the system of unilateral action, the exclusive alliances, the spheres of

Mr. Schlesinger is Albert Schweitzer Professor of the Humanities at the City University of New York.

Excerpted by permission from *Foreign Affairs*, October, 1967. Copyright held by the Council on Foreign Relations, Inc., New York.

influence, the balances of power, and all the other expedients that have been tried for centuries—and have always failed."

Whenever Roosevelt backslid, he had at his side that Wilsonian fundamentalist, Secretary of State Cordell Hull, to recall him to the pure faith. . . . Remembering the corruption of the Wilsonian vision by the secret treaties of the First World War, Hull was determined to prevent any sphere-of-influence nonsense after the Second World War . . . . In adopting the universalist view, Roosevelt and Hull were not indulging personal hobbies. Sumner Welles, Adolf Berle, Averell Harriman, Charles Bohlen—all, if with a variety of nuances, opposed the sphere-of-influence approach. And here the State Department was expressing what seems clearly to have been the predominant mood of the American people, so long mistrustful of European power politics. The Republicans shared the true faith. John Foster Dulles argued that the great threat to peace after the war would lie in the revival of sphere-of-influence thinking . . . .

There seem only to have been three officials in the United States Government who dissented. One was the Secretary of War, Henry L. Stimson, a classical balance-of-power man, who in 1944 opposed the creation of a vacuum in Central Europe by the pastoralization of Germany and in 1945 urged "the settlement of all territorial acquisitions in the shape of defense posts which each of these four powers may deem to be necessary for their own safety" in advance of any effort to establish a peacetime United Nations. Stimson considered the claim of Russia to a preferred position in Eastern Europe as not unreasonable: as he told President Truman, "he thought the Russians perhaps were being more realistic than we were in regard to their own security." Such a position for Russia seemed to him comparable to the preferred American position in Latin America; he even spoke of "our respective orbits." Stimson was therefore skeptical of what he regarded as the prevailing tendency "to hang on to exaggerated views of the Monroe Doctrine and at the same time butt into every question that comes up in Central Europe." Acceptance of spheres of influence seemed to him the way to avoid "a head-on collision."

A second official opponent of universalism was George Kennan, an eloquent advocate from the American Embassy in Moscow of "a prompt and clear recognition of the division of Europe into spheres of influence and of a policy based on the fact of such division." Kennan argued that nothing we could do would possibly alter the course of events in Eastern Europe; that we were deceiving ourselves by supposing that these countries had any future but Russian domination; that we should therefore relinquish Eastern Europe to the Soviet Union and avoid anything which would make things easier for the Russians by giving them economic assistance or by sharing moral responsibility for their actions.

A third voice within the government against universalism was (at least after the war) Henry A. Wallace. As Secretary of Commerce, he stated the sphere-of-influence case with trenchancy in the famous Madison Square Garden speech of September 1946 which led to his dismissal by President Truman:

> On our part, we should recognize that we have no more business in the *political* affairs of Eastern Europe than Russia has in the *political* affairs of Latin America, Western Europe, and the United States. . . . Whether we like it or not, the Russians will try to socialize their sphere of influence just as we try to democratize our sphere of influence. . . . The Russians have no more business stirring up native Communists to political activity in Western Europe, Latin America, and the United States than we have in interfering with the politics of Eastern Europe and Russia.

Stimson, Kennan and Wallace seem to have been alone in the government, however, in taking these views. They were very much minority voices. Meanwhile universalism, rooted in the American legal and moral tradition, overwhelmingly backed by contemporary opinion, received successive enshrinements in the Atlantic Charter of 1941, in the Declaration of the United Nations in 1942 and in the Moscow Declaration of 1943.

The Kremlin, on the other hand, thought *only* of spheres of interest; above all, the Russians were determined to protect their frontiers, and especially their border to the west, crossed so often and so bloodily in the dark course of their history. These western frontiers lacked natural means of defense—no great oceans, rugged mountains, steaming swamps or impenetrable jungles. The history of Russia had been the history of invasion, the last of which was by now horribly killing up to twenty million of its people. The protocol of Russia therefore meant the enlargement of the area of Russian influence. Kennan himself wrote (in May 1944), "Behind Russia's stubborn expansion lies only the age-old sense of insecurity of a sedentary people reared on an exposed plain in the neighborhood of fierce nomadic peoples," and he called this "urge" a "permanent feature of Russian psychology.". . . .

It is true that, so long as Russian survival appeared to require a second front to relieve the Nazi pressure, Moscow's demand for Eastern Europe was a little muffled. Thus the Soviet government adhered to the Atlantic Charter (though with a significant if obscure reservation about adapting its principles to "the circumstances, needs, and historic peculiarites of particular countries"). Thus it also adhered to the Moscow Declaration of 1943, and Molotov then, with his easy mendacity, even denied that Russia had any desire to divide Europe into spheres of influence. But this was guff, which the Russians were perfectly willing to ladle out if it would keep the Americans, and especially Secretary Hull (who made a strong personal impression at the Moscow conference) happy. "A declaration," as Stalin once observed to Eden, "I regard as algebra, but an agreement as practical arithmetic. I do not wish to decry algebra, but I prefer practical arithmetic."

The more consistent Russian purpose was revealed when Stalin offered the British a straight sphere-of-influence deal at the end of 1941. Britain, he suggested, should recognize the Russian absorption of the Baltic states, part of Finland, eastern Poland and Bessarabia; in return, Russia would support any special British need for bases or security arrangements in Western Europe. There was nothing specifically communist about these ambitions.

If Stalin achieved them, he would be fulfilling an age-old dream of the tsars . . . .

Teheran in December 1943 marked the high point of three-power collaboration. Still, when Churchill asked about Russian territorial interests, Stalin replied a little ominously, "There is no need to speak at the present time about any Soviet desires, but when the time comes we will speak." In the next weeks, there were increasing indications of a Soviet determination to deal unilaterally with

Eastern Europe—so much so that in early February 1944 Hull cabled Harriman in Moscow:

> Matters are rapidly approaching the point where the Soviet Government will have to choose between the development and extension of the foundation of international cooperation as the guiding principle of the postwar world as against the continuance of a unilateral and arbitrary method of dealing with its special problems even though these problems are admittedly of more direct interest to the Soviet Union than to other great powers.

As against this approach, however, Churchill, more tolerant of sphere-of-influence deviations, soon proposed that, with the impending liberation of the Balkans, Russia should run things in Rumania and Britain in Greece. Hull strongly opposed this suggestion but made the mistake of leaving Washington for a few days; and Roosevelt, momentarily free from his Wilsonian conscience, yielded to Churchill's plea for a three-months' trial. Hull resumed the fight on his return, and Churchill postponed the matter. . . .

The problem, as Harriman had earlier told Harry Hopkins, was "to strengthen the hands of those around Stalin who want to play the game along our lines." The way to do this, he now told Hull, was to

> be understanding of their sensitivity, meet them much more than half way, encourage them and support them wherever we can, and yet oppose them promptly with the greatest of firmness where we see them going wrong. . . . The only way we can eventually come to an understanding with the Soviet Union on the question of non-interference in the internal affairs of other countries is for us to take a definite interest in the solution of the problems of each individual country as they arise.

As against Harriman's sophisticated universalist strategy, however, Churchill, increasingly fearful of the consequences of unrestrained competition in Eastern Europe, decided in early October to carry his sphere-of-influence proposal directly to Moscow. Roosevelt was at first content to have Churchill speak for him too and even prepared a cable to that effect. But Hopkins, a more rigorous universalist, took it upon himself to stop the cable and warn Roosevelt of its possible implications. Eventually Roosevelt sent a message to Harriman in Moscow emphasizing that he expected to "retain complete freedom of action after this conference is over." It was now that Churchill quickly proposed—and Stalin as quickly accepted—the celebrated division of southeastern Europe: ending (after further haggling between Eden and Molotov) with 90 percent Soviet predominance in Rumania, 80 percent in Bulgaria and Hungary, fifty-fifty in Jugoslavia, 90 percent British predominance in Greece.

Churchill in discussing this with Harriman used the phrase "spheres of influence." But he insisted that these were only "immediate wartime arrangements" and received a highly general blessing from Roosevelt. Yet, whatever Churchill intended, there is reason to believe that Stalin construed the percentages as an agreement, not a declaration; as practical arithmetic, not algebra. For Stalin, it should be understood, the sphere-of-influence idea did not mean that he would abandon all efforts to spread communism in some other nation's sphere; it did mean that, if he tried this and the other side cracked down, he could not feel he had serious cause for complaint. As Kennan wrote to Harriman at the end of 1944:

> As far as border states are concerned the Soviet government has never ceased to think in terms of spheres of interest. They expect us to support them in whatever action they wish to take in those regions, regardless of whether that action seems to us or to the rest of the world to be right or wrong. . . . I have no doubt that this position is honestly maintained on their part, and that they would be equally prepared to reserve moral judgment on any actions which we might wish to carry out, i.e., in the Caribbean area.

. . . It is not unreasonable to suppose that Stalin would have been satisfied at the end of the war to secure what Kennan has called "a protective glacis along Russia's western border," and that, in exchange for a free hand in Eastern Europe, he was prepared to give the British and Americans equally free hands in their zones of vital interest, including in nations as close to Russia as Greece (for the British) and, very probably—or at least so the Jugoslavs believe—China (for the United States). In other words, his initial objectives were very probably not world conquest but Russian security.

It is now pertinent to inquire why the United States rejected the idea of stabilizing the world by division into spheres of influence and insisted on an East European strategy. One should warn against rushing to the conclusion that it was all a row between hard-nosed, balance-of-power realists and starry-eyed Wilsonians. Roosevelt, Hopkins, Welles, Harriman, Bohlen, Berle, Dulles and other universalists were tough and serious men. Why then did they rebuff the sphere-of-influence solution?

The first reason is that they regarded this solution as containing within itself the seeds of a third world war. The balance-of-power idea seemed inherently unstable. It had always broken down in the past. It held out to each power the permanent temptation to try to alter the balance in its own favor, and it built this temptation into the international order. . . . The Americans were perfectly ready to acknowledge that Russia was entitled to convincing assurance of her national security—but not this way. "I could sympathize fully with Stalin's desire to protect his western borders from future attack," as Hull put it. "But I felt that this security could best be obtained through a strong postwar peace organization."

Hull's remark suggests the second objection: that the sphere-of-influence approach would, in the words of the State Department in 1945, "militate against the establishment and effective functioning of a broader system of general security in which all countries will have their part." The United Nations, in short, was seen as the alternative to the balance of power. Nor did the universalists see any necessary incompatibility between the Russian desire for "friendly governments" on its frontier and the American desire for self-determination in Eastern Europe. Before Yalta the State Department judged the general mood of Europe as "to the left and strongly in favor of far-reaching economic and social reforms, but not, however, in favor of a left-wing totalitarian regime to achieve these reforms." Governments in Eastern Europe could be sufficiently to the left "to allay Soviet suspicions" but sufficiently representative "of the center and *petit bourgeois* elements" not to seem a prelude to communist dictatorship. The American criteria were therefore that the government "should be dedicated to the preservation of civil liberties" and "should favor social and economic reforms." A string of New Deal states—of Finlands and Czechoslovakias—seemed a reasonable compromise solution.

Third, the universalists feared that the sphere-of-interest approach would be what Hull termed "a haven for the isolationists," who would advocate America's participation in Western Hemisphere affairs on condition that it did not participate in European or Asian affairs. Hull also feared that spheres of interest would lead to "closed trade areas or discriminatory systems" and thus defeat his cherished dream of a low-tariff, freely trading world.

Fourth, the sphere-of-interest solution meant the betrayal of the principles for which the Second World War was being fought—the Atlantic Charter, the Four Freedoms, the Declaration of the United Nations. Poland summed up the problem. Britain, having gone to war to defend the independence of Poland from the Germans, could not easily conclude the war by surrendering the independence of Poland to the Russians. Thus, as Hopkins told Stalin after Roosevelt's death in 1945, Poland had "become the symbol of our ability to work out problems with the Soviet Union." Nor could American liberals in general watch with equanimity while the police state spread into countries which, if they had mostly not been real democracies, had mostly not been tyrannies either. . . .

Fifth, the sphere-of-influence solution would create difficult domestic problems in American politics. Roosevelt was aware of the six million or more Polish votes in the 1944 election; even more acutely, he was aware of the broader and deeper attack which would follow if, after going to war to stop the Nazi conquest of Europe, he permitted the war to end with the communist conquest of Eastern Europe. . . .

Sixth, if the Russians were allowed to overrun Eastern Europe without argument, would that satisfy them? Even Kennan, in a dispatch of May 1944, admitted that the "urge" had dreadful potentialities: "If initially successful, will it know where to stop? Will it not be inexorably carried forward, by its very nature, in a struggle to reach the whole—to attain complete mastery of the shores of the Atlantic and the Pacific?" His own answer was that there were inherent limits to the Russian capacity to expand—"that Russia will not have an easy time in maintaining the power which it has seized over other people in Eastern and Central Europe unless it receives both moral and material assistance from the West." Subsequent developments have vindicated Kennan's argument. . . . But, given Russia's success in maintaining centralized control over the international communist movement for a quarter of a century, who in 1944 could have had much confidence in the idea of communist revolts against Moscow?

Most of those involved therefore rejected Kennan's answer and stayed with his question. If the West turned its back on Eastern Europe, the higher probability, in their view, was that the Russians would use their security zone, not just for defensive purposes, but as a springboard from which to mount an attack on Western Europe, now shattered by war, a vacuum of power awaiting its master. "If the policy is accepted that the Soviet Union has a right to penetrate her immediate neighbors for security," Harriman said in 1944, "penetration of the next immediate neighbors becomes at a certain time equally logical." If a row with Russia were inevitable, every consideration of prudence dictated that it should take place in Eastern rather than Western Europe.

Thus idealism and realism joined in opposition to the sphere-of-influence solution. The consequence was a determination to assert an American interest in the postwar destiny of all nations, including those of Eastern Europe. In the message which Roosevelt and Hopkins drafted after Hopkins had stopped Roosevelt's initial cable authorizing Churchill to speak for the United States at the Moscow meeting of October 1944, Roosevelt now said, "There is in this global war literally no question, either military or political, in which the United States is not interested." After Roosevelt's death Hopkins repeated the point to Stalin: "The cardinal basis of President Roosevelt's policy which the American people had fully supported had been the concept that the interests of the U.S. were worldwide and not confined to North and South America and the Pacific Ocean."

For better or worse, this was the American position. It is now necessary to attempt the imaginative leap and consider the impact of this position on the leaders of the Soviet Union who, also for better or for worse, had reached the bitter conclusion that the survival of their country depended on their unchallenged control of the corridors through which enemies had so often invaded their homeland. They could claim to have been keeping their own side of the sphere-of-influence bargain. Of course, they were working to capture the resistance movements of Western Europe; indeed, with the appointment of Oumansky as Ambassador to Mexico they were even beginning to enlarge underground operations in the Western Hemisphere. But, from their viewpoint, if the West permitted this, the more fools they; and, if the West stopped it, it was within their right to do so. In overt political matters the Russians were scrupulously playing the game. They had watched in silence while the British shot down communists in Greece. In Jugoslavia Stalin was urging Tito (as Djilas later revealed) to keep King Peter. They had not only acknowledged Western preëminence in Italy but had recognized the Badoglio régime; the Italian Communists had even voted (against the Socialists and the Liberals) for the renewal of the Lateran Pacts.

They would not regard anti-communist action in a Western zone as a *casus belli;* and they expected reciprocal license to assert their own authority in the East. But the principle of self-determination was carrying the United States into a deeper entanglement in Eastern Europe than the Soviet Union claimed as a right (whatever it was doing underground) in the affairs of Italy, Greece or China. When the Russians now exercised in Eastern Europe the same brutal control they were prepared to have Washington exercise in the American sphere of influence, the American protests, given the paranoia produced alike by Russian history and Leninist ideology, no doubt seemed not only an act of hypocrisy but a threat to security. To the Russians, a stroll into the neighborhood easily became a plot to burn down the house.

. . . It is not unusual to suspect one's adversary of doing what one is already doing oneself. At the same time, the cruelty with which the Russians executed their idea of spheres of influence—in a sense, perhaps, an unwitting cruelty, since Stalin treated the East Europeans no worse than he had treated the Russians in the thirties— discouraged the West from accepting the equation (for example, Italy = Rumania) which seemed so self-evident to the Kremlin.

So Moscow very probably, and not unnaturally, perceived the emphasis on self-determination as a systematic and deliberate pressure on Russia's western frontiers. Moreover, the restoration of capitalism to countries freed at frightful cost by the Red Army no doubt struck the Russians as the betrayal of the principles for which *they* were fighting. "That they, the victors," Isaac Deutscher has suggested, "should now preserve an order from which they had experienced nothing but hostility, and could expect nothing but hostility . . . would have been the most miserable anti-climax to their great 'war of liberation.'" By 1944 Poland was the critical issue. . . . While the West saw the point of Stalin's demand for a "friendly government" in Warsaw, the American insistence on the sovereign virtues of free elections created an insoluble problem in those countries, like Poland (and Rumania) where free elections would almost certainly produce anti-Soviet governments.

The Russians thus may well have estimated the Western pressures as calculated to encourage their enemies in Eastern Europe and to defeat their own minimum objective of a protective glacis. Everything still hung, however, on the course of military operations. The wartime collaboration had been created by one thing, and one thing alone: the threat of Nazi victory. So long as this threat was real, so was the collaboration. In late December 1944, von Rundstedt launched his counter-offensive in the Ardennes. A few weeks later, when Roosevelt, Churchill and Stalin gathered in the Crimea, it was in the shadow of this last considerable explosion of German power. The meeting at Yalta was still dominated by the mood of war.

Yalta remains something of an historical perplexity—less, from the perspective of 1967, because of a mythical American deference to the sphere-of-influence thesis than because of the documentable Russian deference to the universalist thesis. Why should Stalin in 1945 have accepted the Declaration on Liberated Europe and an agreement on Poland pledging that "the three governments will jointly" act to assure "free elections of governments responsive to the will of the people"? There are several probable answers: that the war was not over and the Russians still wanted the Americans to intensify their military effort in the West; that one clause in the Declaration premised action on "the opinion of the three governments" and thus implied a Soviet veto, though the Polish agreement was more definite; most of all that the universalist algebra of the Declaration was plainly in Stalin's mind to be construed in terms of the practical arithmetic of his sphere-of-influence agreement with Churchill the previous October. Stalin's assurance to Churchill at Yalta that a proposed Russian amendment to the Declaration would not apply to Greece makes it clear that Roosevelt's pieties did not, in Stalin's mind, nullify Churchill's percentages . . . . In the weeks after Yalta, the military situation changed with great rapidity. As the Nazi threat declined, so too did the need for coöperation. The Soviet Union, feeling itself menaced by the American idea of self-determination and the borderlands diplomacy to which it was leading, skeptical whether the United Nations would protect its frontiers as reliably as its own domination in Eastern Europe, began to fulfill its security requirements unilaterally.

In March Stalin expressed his evaluation of the United Nations by rejecting Roosevelt's plea that Molotov come to the San Francisco conference, if only for the opening sessions. In the next weeks the Russians emphatically and crudely worked their will in Eastern Europe, above all in the test country of Poland. They were ignoring the Declaration on Liberated Europe, ignoring the Atlantic Charter, self-determination, human freedom and everything else the Americans considered essential for a stable peace . . . .

At the same time, the Russians also began to mobilize communist resources in the United States itself to block American universalism. In April 1945 Jacques Duclos, who had been the Comintern official responsible for the Western communist parties, launched in *Cahiers du Communisme* an uncompromising attack on the policy of the American Communist Party. Duclos sharply condemned the revisionism of Earl Browder, the American Communist leader . . . The excommunication of Browderism was plainly the Politburo's considered reaction to the impending defeat of Germany; it was a signal to the communist parties of the West that they should recover their identity; it was Moscow's alert to communists everywhere that they should prepare for new policies in the postwar world.

The Duclos piece obviously could not have been planned and written much later than the Yalta conference—that is, well before a number of events which revisionists now cite in order to demonstrate American responsibility for the Cold War: before Allen Dulles, for example, began to negotiate the surrender of the German armies in Italy (the episode which provoked Stalin to charge Roosevelt with seeking a separate peace and provoked Roosevelt to denounce the "vile misrepresentations" of Stalin's informants); well before Roosevelt died; many months before the testing of the atomic bomb; even more months before Truman ordered that the bomb be dropped on Japan. William Z. Foster, who soon replaced Browder as the leader of the American Communist Party and embodied the new Moscow line, later boasted of having said in January 1944, "A post-war Roosevelt administration would continue to be, as it is now, an imperialist government." With ancient suspicions revived by the American insistence on universalism, this was no doubt the conclusion which the Russians were reaching at the same time. . . .

The atmosphere of mutual suspicion was beginning to rise. In January 1945 Molotov formally proposed that the United States grant Russia a $6 billion credit for postwar reconstruction. With characteristic tact he explained that he was doing this as a favor to save America from a postwar depression. The proposal seems to have been diffidently made and diffidently received. Roosevelt requested that the matter "not be pressed further" on the American side until he had a chance to talk with Stalin; but the Russians did not follow it up either at Yalta in February (save for a single glancing reference) or during the Stalin-Hopkins talks in May or at Potsdam. Finally the proposal was renewed in the very different political atmosphere of August. This time Washington inexplicably mislaid the request during the transfer of the records of the Foreign Economic Administration to the State Department. It did not turn up again until March 1946. Of course this was impossible for the Russians to believe; it is hard enough even for those acquainted with the capacity of the American government for incompetence to believe; and it only strengthened Soviet suspicions of American purposes.

The American credit was one conceivable form of Western contribution to Russian reconstruction. Another was lend-lease, and the possibility of reconstruction aid under the lend-lease protocol had already been discussed in 1944. But in May 1945 Russia, like Britain, suffered from Truman's abrupt termination of lend-lease shipments—"unfortunate and even brutal," Stalin told Hopkins, adding that, if it was "designed as pressure on the Russians in order to soften them up, then it was a fundamental mistake." A third form was German reparations. Here Stalin in demanding $10 billion in reparations for the Soviet Union made his strongest fight at Yalta. Roosevelt, while agreeing essentially with Churchill's opposition, tried to postpone the matter by accepting the Soviet figure as a "basis for discussion"—a formula which led to future misunderstanding. In short, the Russian hope for major Western assistance in postwar reconstruction foundered on three events which the Kremlin could well have interpreted respectively as deliberate sabotage (the loan request), blackmail (lend-lease cancellation) and pro-Germanism (reparations).

Actually the American attempt to settle the fourth lend-lease protocol was generous and the Russians for their own reasons declined to come to an agreement. It is not clear, though, that satisfying Moscow on any of these financial scores would have made much essential difference. It might have persuaded some doves in the Kremlin that the U.S. government was genuinely friendly; it might have persuaded some hawks that the American anxiety for Soviet friendship was such that Moscow could do as it wished without inviting challenge from the United States. It would, in short, merely have reinforced both sides of the Kremlin debate; it would hardly have reversed deeper tendencies toward the deterioration of political relationships. Economic deals were surely subordinate to the quality of mutual political confidence; and here, in the months after Yalta, the decay was steady.

The Cold War had now begun. It was the product not of a decision but of a dilemma. Each side felt compelled to adopt policies which the other could not but regard as a threat to the principles of the peace. Each then felt compelled to undertake defensive measures. Thus the Russians saw no choice but to consolidate their security in Eastern Europe. The Americans, regarding Eastern Europe as the first step toward Western Europe, responded by asserting their interest in the zone the Russians deemed vital to their security. The Russians concluded that the West was resuming its old course of capitalist encirclement; that it was purposefully laying the foundation for anti-Soviet régimes in the area defined by the blood of centuries as crucial to Russian survival. Each side believed with passion that future international stability depended on the success of its own conception of world order. Each side, in pursuing its own clearly indicated and deeply cherished principles, was only confirming the fear of the other that it was bent on aggression.

Very soon the process began to acquire a cumulative momentum. The impending collapse of Germany thus provoked new troubles: the Russians, for example, sincerely feared that the West was planning a separate surrender of the German armies in Italy in a way which would release troops for Hitler's eastern front, as they subsequently feared that the Nazis might succeed in surrendering Berlin to the West. This was the context in which the atomic bomb now appeared. Though the revisionist argument that Truman dropped the bomb less to defeat Japan than to intimidate Russia is not convincing, this thought unquestionably appealed to some in Washington as at least an advantageous side-effect of Hiroshima.

So the machinery of suspicion and counter-suspicion, action and counter-action, was set in motion. But, given relations among traditional national states, there was still no reason, even with all the postwar jostling, why this should not have remained a manageable situation. What made it unmanageable, what caused the rapid escalation of the Cold War and in another two years completed the division of Europe, was a set of considerations which this account has thus far excluded.

Up to this point, the discussion has considered the schism within the wartime coalition as if it were entirely the result of disagreements among national states. Assuming this framework, there was unquestionably a failure of communication between America and Russia, a misperception of signals and, as time went on, a mounting tendency to ascribe ominous motives to the other side. It seems hard, for example, to deny that American postwar policy created genuine difficulties for the Russians and even assumed a threatening aspect for them. All this the revisionists have rightly and usefully emphasized.

But the great omission of the revisionists—and also the fundamental explanation of the speed with which the Cold War escalated—lies precisely in the fact that the Soviet Union was *not* a traditional national state.[1] This is where the "mirror image," invoked by some psychologists, falls down. For the Soviet Union was

---

[1] This is the classical revisionist fallacy—the assumption of the rationality, or at least of the traditionalism, of states where ideology and social organization have created a different range of motives. So the Second World War revisionists omit the totalitarian dynamism of Nazism and the fanaticism of Hitler, as the Civil War revisionists omit the fact that the slavery system was producing a doctrinaire closed society in the American South. For a consideration of some of these issues, see "The Causes of the Civil War: A Note on Historical Sentimentalism" in my "The Politics of Hope" (Boston, 1963).

a phenomenon very different from America or Britain: it was a totalitarian state, endowed with an all-explanatory, all-consuming ideology, committed to the infallibility of government and party, still in a somewhat messianic mood, equating dissent with treason, and ruled by a dictator who, for all his quite extraordinary abilities, had his paranoid moments.

Marxism-Leninism gave the Russian leaders a view of the world according to which all societies were inexorably destined to proceed along appointed roads by appointed stages until they achieved the classless nirvana. Moreover, given the resistance of the capitalists to this development, the existence of any non-communist state was *by definition* a threat to the Soviet Union. "As long as capitalism and socialism exist," Lenin wrote, "we cannot live in peace: in the end, one or the other will triumph—a funeral dirge will be sung either over the Soviet Republic or over world capitalism."

Stalin and his associates, whatever Roosevelt or Truman did or failed to do, were bound to regard the United States as the enemy, not because of this deed or that, but because of the primordial fact that America was the leading capitalist power and thus, by Leninist syllogism, unappeasably hostile, driven by the logic of its system to oppose, encircle and destroy Soviet Russia. Nothing the United States could have done in 1944–45 would have abolished this mistrust, required and sanctified as it was by Marxist gospel— nothing short of the conversion of the United States into a Stalinist despotism; and even this would not have sufficed, as the experience of Jugoslavia and China soon showed, unless it were accompanied by total subservience to Moscow. So long as the United States remained a capitalist democracy, no American policy, given Moscow's theology, could hope to win basic Soviet confidence, and every American action was poisoned from the source. So long as the Soviet Union remained a messianic state, ideology compelled a steady expansion of communist power.

It is easy, of course, to exaggerate the capacity of ideology to control events. The tension of acting according to revolutionary abstractions is too much for most nations to sustain over a long period: that is why Mao Tse-tung has launched his Cultural Revolution, hoping thereby to create a permanent revolutionary mood and save Chinese communism from the degeneration which, in his view, has overtaken Russian communism. Still, as any revolution grows older, normal human and social motives will increasingly reassert themselves. In due course, we can be sure, Leninism will be about as effective in governing the daily lives of Russians as Christianity is in governing the daily lives of Americans. Like the Ten Commandments and the Sermon on the Mount, the Leninist verities will increasingly become platitudes for ritual observance, not guides to secular decision. There can be no worse fallacy (even if respectable people practiced it diligently for a season in the United States) than that of drawing from a nation's ideology permanent conclusions about its behavior . . . .

Paradoxically, of the forces capable of bringing about a modification of ideology, the most practical and effective was the Soviet dictatorship itself. If Stalin was an ideologist, he was also a pragmatist. If he saw everything through the lenses of Marxism-Leninism, he also, as the infallible expositor of the faith, could reinterpret Marxism-Leninism to justify anything he wanted to do at any given moment. No doubt Roosevelt's ignorance of Marxism-Leninism was inexcusable and led to grievous miscalculations. But Roosevelt's efforts to work on and through Stalin were not so hopelessly naïve as it used to be fashionable to think. With the extraordinary instinct of a great political leader, Roosevelt intuitively understood that Stalin was the *only* lever available to the West against the Leninist ideology and the Soviet system. If Stalin could be reached, then alone was there a chance of getting the Russians to act contrary to the prescriptions of their faith. The best evidence is that Roosevelt retained a certain capacity to influence Stalin to the end; the nominal Soviet acquiescence in American universalism as late as Yalta was perhaps an indication of that. It is in this way that the death of Roosevelt was crucial—not in the vulgar sense that his policy was then reversed by his successor, which did not happen, but in the sense that no other American could hope to have the restraining impact on Stalin which Roosevelt might for a while have had.

Stalin alone could have made any difference. Yet Stalin, in spite of the impression of sobriety and realism he made on Westerners who saw him during the Second World War, was plainly a man of deep and morbid obsessions and compulsions . . . . His paranoia, probably set off by the suicide of his wife in 1932, led to the terrible purges of the mid-thirties and the wanton murder of thousands of his Bolshevik comrades . . . . The madness, so rigidly controlled for a time, burst out with new and shocking intensity in the postwar years. . . . A revisionist fallacy has been to treat Stalin as just another Realpolitik statesman, as Second World War revisionists see Hitler as just another Stresemann or Bismarck. But the record makes it clear that in the end nothing could satisfy Stalin's paranoia. His own associates failed. Why does anyone suppose that any conceivable American policy would have succeeded?

An analysis of the origins of the Cold War which leaves out these factors—the intransigence of Leninist ideology, the sinister dynamics of a totalitarian society and the madness of Stalin—is obviously incomplete. It was these factors which made it hard for the West to accept the thesis that Russia was moved only by a desire to protect its security and would be satisfied by the control of Eastern Europe; it was these factors which charged the debate between universalism and spheres of influence with apocalyptic potentiality.

Leninism and totalitarianism created a structure of thought and behavior which made postwar collaboration between Russia and America—in any normal sense of civilized intercourse between national states—inherently impossible. The Soviet dictatorship of 1945 simply could not have survived such a collaboration. Indeed, nearly a quarter-century later, the Soviet régime, though it has meanwhile moved a good distance, could still hardly survive it without risking the release inside Russia of energies profoundly opposed to communist despotism. As for Stalin, he may have represented the only force in 1945 capable of overcoming Stalinism, but the very traits which enabled him to win absolute power expressed terrifying instabilities of mind and temperament and hardly offered a solid foundation for a peaceful world.

The difference between America and Russia in 1945 was that some Americans fundamentally believed that, over a long run, a modus vivendi with Russia was possible; while the Russians, so far as one can tell, believed in no more than a short-run modus vivendi with the United States.

Harriman and Kennan, this narrative has made clear, took the lead in warning Washington about the difficulties of short-run dealings with the Soviet Union. But both argued that, if the United States developed a rational policy and stuck to it, there would be, after long and rough passages, the prospect of eventual clearing. "I am, as you know," Harriman cabled Washington in early April, "a most earnest advocate of the closest possible understanding with the Soviet Union so that what I am saying relates only to how best to attain such understanding." Kennan has similarly made it clear that the function of his containment policy was "to tide us over a difficult time and bring us to the point where we could discuss effectively with the Russians the dangers and drawbacks this status quo involved, and to arrange with them for its peaceful replacement by a better and sounder one." The subsequent careers of both men attest to the honesty of these statements.

There is no corresponding evidence on the Russian side that anyone seriously sought a modus vivendi in these terms. Stalin's choice was whether his long-term ideological and national interests would be better served by a short-run truce with the West or by an immediate resumption of pressure. In October 1945 Stalin indicated to Harriman at Sochi that he planned to adopt the second course— that the Soviet Union was going isolationist. No doubt the succession of problems with the United States contributed to this decision, but the basic causes most probably lay elsewhere: in the developing situations in Eastern Europe, in Western Europe and in the United States.

In Eastern Europe, Stalin was still for a moment experimenting with techniques of control. But he must by now have begun to conclude that he had underestimated the hostility of the people to Russian dominion. The Hungarian elections in November would finally convince him that the Yalta formula was a road to anti-Soviet governments. At the same time, he was feeling more strongly than ever a sense of his opportunities in Western Europe. The other half of the Continent lay unexpectedly before him, politically demoralized, economically prostrate, militarily defenseless. The hunting would be better and safer than he had anticipated. As for the United States, the alacrity of postwar demobilization must have recalled Roosevelt's offhand remark at Yalta that "two years would be the limit" for keeping American troops in Europe. And, despite Dr.

Eugene Varga's doubts about the imminence of American economic breakdown, Marxist theology assured Stalin that the United States was heading into a bitter postwar depression and would be consumed with its own problems. If the condition of Eastern Europe made unilateral action seem essential in the interests of Russian security, the condition of Western Europe and the United States offered new temptations for communist expansion. The Cold War was now in full swing.

It still had its year of modulations and accommodations. Secretary Byrnes conducted his long and fruitless campaign to persuade the Russians that America only sought governments in Eastern Europe "both friendly to the Soviet Union and representative of all the democratic elements of the country." Crises were surmounted in Trieste and Iran. Secretary Marshall evidently did not give up hope of a modus vivendi until the Moscow conference of foreign secretaries of March 1947. Even then, the Soviet Union was invited to participate in the Marshall Plan.

The point of no return came on July 2, 1947, when Molotov, after bringing 89 technical specialists with him to Paris and evincing initial interest in the project for European reconstruction, received the hot flash from the Kremlin, denounced the whole idea and walked out of the conference. For the next fifteen years the Cold War raged unabated, passing out of historical ambiguity into the realm of good versus evil and breeding on both sides simplifications, stereotypes and self-serving absolutes, often couched in interchangeable phrases. Under the pressure even America, for a deplorable decade, forsook its pragmatic and pluralist traditions, posed as God's appointed messenger to ignorant and sinful man and followed the Soviet example in looking to a world remade in its own image.

In retrospect, if it is impossible to see the Cold War as a case of American aggression and Russian response, it is also hard to see it as a pure case of Russian aggression and American response. "In what is truly tragic," wrote Hegel, "there must be valid moral powers on both the sides which come into collision. . . . Both suffer loss and yet both are mutually justified." In this sense, the Cold War had its tragic elements. The question remains whether it was an instance of Greek tragedy—as Auden has called it, "the tragedy of necessity," where the feeling aroused in the spectator is "What a pity it had to be this way"—or of Christian tragedy, "the tragedy of possibility," where the feeling aroused is "What a pity it was this way when it might have been otherwise."

Once something has happened, the historian is tempted to assume that it had to happen; but this may often be a highly unphilosophical assumption. The Cold War could have been avoided only if the Soviet Union had not been possessed by convictions both of the infallibility of the communist word and of the inevitability of a communist world. These convictions transformed an impasse between national states into a religious war, a tragedy of possibility into one of necessity. One might wish that America had preserved the poise and proportion of the first years of the Cold War and had not in time succumbed to its own forms of self-righteousness. But the most rational of American policies could hardly have averted the Cold War. Only today, as Russia begins to recede from its messianic mission and to accept, in practice if not yet in principle, the permanence of the world of diversity, only now can the hope flicker that this long, dreary, costly contest may at last be taking on forms less dramatic, less obsessive and less dangerous to the future of mankind.

JOHN SPANIER
American Foreign Policy Since World War II

THE AMERICAN DREAM of postwar peace and Big Three cooperation was to be shattered as the Soviet Union expanded into Eastern and Central Europe, imposing its control upon Poland, Hungary, Bulgaria, Romania, and Albania. (Yugoslavia was already under the Communist control of Marshal Tito, and Czechoslovakia was living under the shadow of the Red Army.) In each of these nations of Eastern Europe where the Russians had their troops, they unilaterally established pro-Soviet coalition governments. The key post in these regimes—the ministry of the interior, which usually controlled the police—was in the hands of the Communists. With this decisive level of power in their grasp, it was an easy matter to extend their domination and subvert the independence of these countries. Thus, as the war drew to a close, it became clear that the words of the Yalta Declaration, in which the Russians had committed themselves to free elections and democratic governments in Eastern Europe, meant quite different things to the Russians than to Americans. For the Soviet Union, control of Eastern Europe, and especially Poland, was essential. This area constituted a vital link in her security belt. After two German invasions in less than thirty years, with no natural barriers to protect her, Russia would as a matter of course try to establish "friendly" governments throughout the area. To the Russians, however, "democratic governments" meant Communist governments, and "free elections" meant elections from which parties not favorable to the Communists were barred. The peace treaties with the former German satellite states (Hungary, Bulgaria, Romania), which were painfully negotiated by the victors in a series of foreign ministers' conferences during 1945 and 1946, could not loosen the tight Soviet grip on what were by now Russian satellite states. Thus a clash with the United States was unavoidable. She, too, wished the Soviet Union to have "friendly"

Mr. Spanier is Professor of Political Science and Director of the Institute of International Relations at the University of Florida.

Excerpted from *American Foreign Policy Since World War II* by John Spanier © 1968 Frederick A. Praeger, Inc. by permission of Frederick A. Praeger, Inc.

governments on her borders, but Washington insisted on taking the term "free elections" seriously. Yet such elections would have resulted in anti-Communist governments. And this the Soviets could not permit. . . .

Thus the cold war grew out of the interactions between traditional power politics and the nature of the Soviet regime. The power vacuum created by Germany's defeat provided the opening for Soviet power to fill, and Communist ideology made a clash inevitable. Because democratic principles could not be extended beyond Western power, Russian dominance in the Balkans and Poland became firmly established, and Soviet power now lapped the shores of the Aegean, the Straits of Constantinople, and—through its close relationship with Yugoslavia—the Adriatic.

Greece, Turkey, and Iran were the first stages beyond the confines of the Red Army to feel the resulting expansionist pressure of the Soviet Union. In the period from the end of the war to early 1947, the Russians attempted to effect a major breakthrough into the Middle East. Every would-be world conqueror—Napoleon, Kaiser Wilhelm II, and Hitler, to mention only a few of the more recent ones—has tried to become master of this area. Napoleon called the Middle East the key to the world, and well he might, for the area links Europe, Africa, and Asia. The power that dominates the Middle East is in an excellent position to expand into North Africa and South Asia, and thereby gain control of the world-island. . . .

In all these situations, the American Government was suddenly confronted with the need for action to support Britain, the traditional guardian of this area against encroachment. In the case of Iran, the United States and Britain delivered firm statements which strongly implied that the two countries would use force to defend Iran. The Soviet response in late March, 1946, was the announcement that the Red Army would be withdrawn during the next five to six weeks. In the Turkish case, the United States sent a naval task force into the Mediterranean immediately after the receipt of the Soviet note on August 7. Twelve days later, the United States replied to the note by rejecting the Russian demand to share sole responsibility for the defense of the Straits with Turkey. Britain sent a similar reply. The Greek situation had not yet come to a head, and the need for American action could be postponed for a while longer. But it should be pointed out that the Administration's actions in Iran and Turkey were merely swift reactions to immediate crises. They were not the product of an over-all American strategy. Such a coherent strategy could only arise from a new assessment of Soviet foreign policy.

THE STRATEGY OF CONTAINMENT

A period of eighteen months passed before the United States undertook that reassessment—from the surrender of Japan on September 2, 1945, until the announcement of the Truman Doctrine on March 12, 1947. Perhaps such a reevaluation could not have been made any more quickly. Public opinion in a democratic country does not normally shift drastically overnight. It would have been too much to expect the American public to change suddenly from an attitude of friendliness toward the Soviet Union—inspired largely by the picture of Russian wartime bravery and endurance and by hopes for peaceful postwar cooperation—to a hostile mood. The American "reservoir of goodwill" for the Soviet Union could not be emptied that quickly. Moreover, the desire for peace was too strong. The United States wished only to be left alone to preoccupy itself once more with domestic affairs. The end of the war signaled the end of power politics and the restoration of normal peacetime harmony among nations. In response to this expectation, the public demanded a speedy demobilization. The armed forces were thus reduced to completely inadequate levels of strength. In May, 1945, at the end of the war with Germany, the United States had an army of 3.5 million men organized into 68 divisions in Europe, supported by 149 air groups. Our allies supplied another 47 divisions. By March, 1946, only ten months later, the United States had only 400,000 troops left, mainly new recruits; the homeland reserve was six battalions. Further reductions in Army strength followed. Air Force and Navy cuts duplicated this same pattern. . . .

Three positions became clear during this period. At one extreme stood that old realist Winston Churchill. At the end of the European war, he had counseled against the withdrawal of American troops. He had insisted that they stay, together with British troops, in order to force the Soviet Union to live up to its Yalta obligations regarding free elections in Eastern Europe and the withdrawal of the Red Army from Eastern Germany. The United States had rejected Churchill's plea. In early 1946, at Fulton, Missouri, Churchill took his case directly to the American public. The Soviet Union, he asserted, was an expansionist state. "From Stettin in the Baltic to Trieste in the Adriatic, an iron curtain has descended across the continent. Behind that line lie all the capitals of the ancient states of Central and Eastern Europe. Warsaw, Berlin, Prague, Vienna, Budapest, Belgrade, Bucharest, and Sofia, all the famous cities and populations around them lie in the Soviet sphere and all are subject in one form or another, not only to Soviet influence but to a very high and increasing measure of control from Moscow." Churchill did not believe that the Russians wanted war: "What they desire is the fruits of war and the indefinite expansion of their power and doctrines." This could be prevented only by the opposing power of the British Commonwealth and the United States. Churchill, in short, said bluntly that the cold war had begun, that Americans must recognize this fact and give up their dreams of Big Three unity in the United Nations. International organization was no substitute for the balance of power. "Our difficulties and dangers will not be removed by closing our eyes to them. They will not be removed by mere waiting to see what happens; nor will they be relieved by a policy of appeasement." An alliance of the English-speaking peoples was the prerequisite for American and British security and world peace.

At the other extreme stood Secretary of Commerce Henry Wallace, who felt it was precisely the kind of aggressive attitude expressed by Churchill that was to blame for Soviet hostility. The United States and Britain had no more business in Eastern Europe than had the Soviet Union in Latin America; to each, the respective area was vital for national security. Western interference in nations bordering on Russia was bound to arouse Soviet suspicion, just as Soviet intervention in countries neighboring on the United States would. "We may not like what Russia does in Eastern Europe," said Wallace. "Her type of land reform, industrial expropriation, and suspension of basic liberties offends the great majority of the people of the United States. But whether we like it or not, the Russians will try to socialize their sphere of influence just as we try to democratize our sphere of influence (including Japan and Western Germany)." The tough attitude that Churchill and other "reactionaries" at home and abroad demanded was precisely the wrong policy; it would only increase international tension. "We must not let British balance-of-power manipulations determine whether and when the United States gets into a war . . . 'getting tough' never bought anything real and lasting—whether for schoolyard bullies or world powers. The tougher we get, the tougher the Russians will get." Only mutual trust would allow the United States and Russia to live together peacefully, and such trust could not be created by an unfriendly American attitude and policy.

The American Government and public wavered between these two positions. The Administration recognized that Big Three cooperation had ended, and it realized that the time when the United States needed to demonstrate goodwill toward the Soviet Union in order to overcome the latter's suspicions had passed. No further concessions would be made to preserve the surface friendship with the Soviet Union. We had tried to gain Russia's amity by being a friend; it was now up to her leaders to demonstrate a similarly friendly attitude toward us as well. Paper agreements, written in such general terms that they actually hid divergent purposes, were no longer regarded as demonstrating such friendship. Something more than paper agreements was needed: Russian words would have to be matched by Russian deeds.

The American Secretary of State, James Byrnes, called this new line the "policy of firmness and patience." This phrase meant that the United States would take a firm position whenever the Soviet Union became intransigent, and that we would not compromise simply in order to reach a quick agreement. This change in official American attitude toward the Soviet Union was not, however, a fundamental one. A firm line was to be followed only on concrete issues. The assumption was that if the United States took a tougher bargaining position and no longer seemed in a hurry to resolve particular points of tension, the Soviet rulers would see the pointlessness of their obduracy and agree to fair compromise solutions of their differences with the United States and the West. In short, American firmness would make the Russians "reasonable." For they were regarded as "unreasonable" merely on particular issues; that this "unreasonableness" might stem from the very nature of the Communist regime had not yet occurred to American policy-makers. They did not yet agree with Churchill's position that the Soviet Government was ideologically hostile to the West and that it would continue to expand until capitalism had been destroyed. The new American position, as one political analyst has aptly summed it up, "meant to most of its exponents that the Soviet Union had to be induced by firmness to play the game in the American way. There was no consistent official suggestion that the United States should begin to play a different game." The prerequisite for such a suggestion was that American policy-makers recognize the revolutionary nature of the Soviet regime.

This recognition came with increasing speed as the Greek crisis reached a peak. By early 1947, it was obvious that the United States would have to play a different game. It was George Kennan, the Foreign Service's foremost expert on the Soviet Union, who first presented the basis of what was to be a new American policy. Kennan's analysis began with a detailed presentation of the Communist outlook on world affairs. In the Soviet leaders' pattern of thought, he said, Russia had no community of interest with the capitalist states; indeed, they saw their relationship with the Western powers in terms of an innate antagonism. Communist ideology had taught them "that the outside world was hostile and that is was their duty eventually to overthrow the political forces beyond their borders. The powerful hands of Russian history and tradition reached up to sustain them in this feeling. Finally, their own aggressive intransigence with respect to the outside world began to find its own reaction . . . It is an undeniable privilege for every man to prove himself right in the thesis that the world is his enemy; for if he reiterates it frequently enough and makes it the background for his conduct, he is bound to be right." According to Kennan, this Soviet hostility was a constant factor; it would continue until the capitalist world had been destroyed: "Basically, the antagonism remains. It is postulated. And from it flow many of the phenomena which we find disturbing in the Kremlin's conduct of foreign policy: the secretiveness, the lack of frankness, the duplicity, the war suspiciousness, and the basic unfriendliness of purpose. . . . These characteristics of the Soviet policy, like the postulates from which they flow, are basic to the *internal* nature of Soviet power, and will be with us . . . until the nature of Soviet power is changed [italics added]." Until that moment, he said, Soviet strategy and objectives would remain the same.

The struggle would thus be a long one. Kennan stressed that Soviet hostility did not mean that the Russians would embark upon a do-or-die program to overthrow capitalism by a fixed date. They had no timetable for conquest. In a brilliant passage, Kennan outlined the Soviet concept of the struggle:

> The Kremlin is under no ideological compulsion to accomplish its purposes in a hurry. Like the Church, it is dealing in ideological concepts which are of a long-term validity, and it can afford to be patient. It has no right to risk the existing achievements of the revolution for the sake of vain baubles of the future. The very teachings of Lenin himself require great caution and flexibility in the pursuit of Communist purposes. Again, these precepts are fortified by the lessons of Russian history: of centuries of obscure battles between nomadic forces over the stretches of a vast unfortified plain. Here caution, circumspection, flexibility, and deception are the valuable qualities; and their value finds natural appreciation in the Russian, or the Oriental mind. Thus the Kremlin has no compunction about retreating in the face of superior force. And being under the compulsion of no timetable, it does not get panicky under the necessity of such a retreat. Its political action is a fluid stream which moves constantly, wherever it is permitted to move, toward a given goal. Its main concern is to make sure that it has filled every nook and cranny available to it in the basin of world power. But if it finds unassailable barriers in its path, it accepts these philosophically and accommodates itself to them. The main thing is that there should always be pressure, increasing constant pressure, toward the desired goal. There is no trace of any feeling in Soviet psychology that the goal must be reached at any given time.

How could the United States counter such a policy—a policy that was always pushing, seeking weak spots, attempting to fill power vacuums? Kennan's answer was that American policy would have to be one of "long-term, patient, but firm and vigilant containment." The United States would find Soviet diplomacy both easier and more difficult to deal with than that of dictators such as Napoleon or Hitler. "On the one hand, it [Soviet policy] is more sensitive to contrary force, more ready to yield on individual sectors of the diplomatic front when that force is felt to be too strong, and thus more rational in the logic and rhetoric of power. On the other hand, it cannot be easily defeated or discouraged by a single victory on the part of its opponents. And the patient persistence by which it is animated means that *it can be effectively countered not by sporadic acts which represent the momentary whims of democratic opinion but only by intelligent long-range policies on the part of Russia's adversaries—policies no less steady in their purpose, and no less variegated and resourceful in their application, than those of the Soviet Union itself* [italics added]." Kennan thus envisaged containment as a test of American democracy to conduct an effective and responsible foreign policy *and* contribute to changes within the Soviet Union which might bring about a moderation of its revolutionary aims. The United States, he emphasized, "has it in its power to increase enormously the strains under which Soviet policy must operate, to force upon the Kremlin a far greater degree of moderation and circumspection than it has had to observe in recent years, and in this way to promote tendencies which must eventually find their outlet in either the breakup or the gradual mellowing of Soviet power. For no mystical, messianic movement—and particularly not that of the Kremlin—can face frustration indefinitely without eventually adjusting itself in one way or another to the logic of that state of affairs." Kennan's theory was thus not so new. He was, in effect, asserting the old thesis that within an authoritarian or totalitarian society there are certain strains and stresses, and that these give rise to frustrations which can only be relieved by being channeled into an aggressive and expansionist foreign policy. Kennan's remedy was to prevent this expansion, thereby aggravating the internal tensions in such a way that they would either destroy the Soviet system or force the Soviet leaders to placate the domestic dissatisfaction. Assuming that the Soviet leaders preferred to remain in power and that they would therefore be compelled to adopt the second course, they would have nò alternative but to moderate their foreign policy. For a relaxation of international tensions was the prerequisite for coping with their domestic problems. Thus, the

Kremlin would have no choice but to surrender its revolutionary aims and arrange a *modus vivendi* with the Western powers—above all, with the United States.

THE TRUMAN DOCTRINE

Whether the United States could meet this Soviet challenge became a pressing question when, on the afternoon of February 21, 1947, the First Secretary of the British Embassy in Washington visited the State Department and handed American officials two notes from His Majesty's Government. One concerned Greece, the other Turkey. In effect, they both stated the same thing: that Britain could no longer meet its traditional responsibilities in those two countries. Since both were on the verge of collapse, the import of the British notes was clear: that a Russian breakthrough could be prevented only by an all-out American commitment.

February 21 was thus a historic day. On that day, Great Britain, the only remaining power in Europe, acknowledged her exhaustion. She had fought Philip II of Spain, Louis XIV of France, Kaiser Wilhelm II and Adolf Hitler of Germany. She had preserved the balance of power which protected the United States for so long that it seemed almost natural for her to continue to do so. But her ability to protect that balance had steadily declined in the twentieth century. Twice she had needed American help. Each time, however, she had fought the longer battle; on neither occasion had the United States entered the war until it became clear that Germany and its allies were too strong for her and that we would have to help her in safeguarding our own security. Now, all of a sudden, there was no power to protect the United States but the United States itself; no one stood between this country and the present threat to its security. All the other major powers of the world had collapsed—except the Soviet Union, which was the second most powerful nation in the world and was wedded to an expansionist ideology. The cold fact of a bipolar world suddenly faced the United States. The country could no longer shirk the responsibilities of its tremendous power.

The immediate crisis suddenly confronting the United States had its locale in the eastern Mediterranean. Direct Soviet pressure on Iran and Turkey had temporarily been successfully resisted. The

Russians had now turned to outflanking these two nations by concentrating their attention on Greece. If Greece collapsed—and all reports from that hapless country indicated that it would fall within a few weeks—it would only be a question of time until Turkey and Iran would crumble before Soviet power. But the fall of Greece would not only affect its neighbors to the east; it would also lead to an increase of Communist pressure on Italy. Italy would then be faced with two Communist states to its east—Yugoslavia and Greece—and with the largest Communist party in Western Europe in its own midst. And to the northwest of Italy lay France, with the second largest Communist party in the West. Thus, the security of all of Western Europe would be endangered as well. The immediate danger, however, remained in the eastern Mediterranean; and the Soviet desire for control over this area was underlined by its demands that the city of Trieste at the head of the Adriatic be yielded to Yugoslavia and that Italy's former colonies of Tripolitania and Eritrea in North Africa be placed under Soviet trusteeship.

The United States had no choice but to act in this situation. The results of inaction were only too clear: the collapse of Europe's flank in the eastern Mediterranean, the establishment of Communist dominance in the Middle East, and a Soviet breakthrough into South Asia and North Africa. The psychological impact upon Europe of such a tremendous Soviet victory over the West would have been disastrous. For Europeans already psychologically demoralized by their sufferings and fall from power and prestige, this would have been the final blow. In short, what was at stake in Greece was America's survival itself.

President Truman was quick to recognize this stark fact. On March 12, 1947, he went before a joint session of Congress and delivered a speech which must rank as one of the most important in American history. The President first outlined the situation in Greece: her lack of natural resources; the cruel German occupation, resulting in widespread destruction; her inability to import the goods she needed for bare subsistence, let alone reconstruction; the Communist efforts to exploit these conditions by spreading political chaos and hindering any economic recovery; and the guerrilla warfare in northern Greece, where the Communist forces were receiving aid from Yugoslavia, Albania, and Bulgaria.

Then Truman came to the heart of his speech. Here he spelled out what was to become known as the Truman Doctrine. The United States, he emphasized, could survive only in a world in which freedom flourished. And we would not realize this objective:

> . . . unless we are willing to help free peoples to maintain their institutions and their national integrity against aggressive movements that seek to impose upon them totalitarian regimes. *This is no more than a frank recognition that totalitarian regimes imposed on free peoples, by direct or indirect aggression, undermine the foundations of international peace and hence the security of the United States* [italics added].
>
> The peoples of a number of countries of the world have recently had totalitarian regimes forced upon them against their will. The Government of the United States has made frequent protests against coercion and intimidation, in violation of the Yalta agreement, in Poland, Romania, and Bulgaria. I must also state that in a number of other countries there have been similar developments.
>
> At the present moment in world history nearly every nation must choose between alternative ways of life. The choice is often not a free one.
>
> One way of life is based upon the will of the majority, and is distinguished by free institutions, representative government, free elections, guarantees of individual liberty, freedom of speech and religion, and freedom from political oppression.
>
> The second way of life is based upon the will of a minority forcibly imposed upon the majority. It relies upon terror and oppression, a controlled press and radio, fixed elections, and the suppression of personal freedoms.
>
> I believe it must be the policy of the United States to support free peoples who are resisting attempted subjugations by armed minorities or by outside pressure.
>
> I believe that we must assist free peoples to work out their own destinies in their own way.
>
> I believe that our help should be primarily through economic and financial aid which is essential to economic stability and orderly political processes.

Stressing the impact of Greece's collapse upon Turkey and the Middle East, as well as upon Europe, the President then brought the Congress and the American people face to face with their responsibility. "Should we fail to aid Greece and Turkey in this fateful hour," he said, "the effect will be far-reaching to the West as well as to the East. We must take immediate and resolute action."

Truman asked Congress to appropriate $400 million for economic aid and military supplies for both countries, and to authorize the dispatch of American civilian and military personnel in order to help the two nations in their tasks of reconstruction and provide their armies with appropriate instruction and training. Truman ended on a grave note:

> This is a serious course upon which we embark.
>
> I would not recommend it except that the alternative is much more serious . . .
>
> The seeds of totalitarian regimes are nurtured by misery and want. They spread and grow in the evil soil of poverty and strife. They reach their full growth when the hope of a people for a better life has died.
>
> We must keep that hope alive.
>
> The free peoples of the world look to us for support in maintaining their freedoms.
>
> If we falter in our leadership, we may endanger the peace of the world—and we shall surely endanger the welfare of our nation.
>
> Great responsibilities have been placed upon us by the swift movement of events.
>
> I am confident that the Congress will face these responsibilities squarely.

The Congress and the American people did. History had once more shown that when a great and democratic people is given decisive and courageous leadership, the people will respond quickly and wisely. Under Truman's leadership, the American public had made a decisive commitment. The United States was now a full participant in the international arena. There could no longer be any retreat. The balance of power was dependent solely upon the United States. The only question was how responsibly and honorably this country would bear its new burden of world leadership.

LOUIS HALLE
The Cold War as History

. . . I HAVE EXAMINED the westward expansion of the Russian
empire at the end of the War, first in abstract general terms, then in
terms of specific events. At the level of abstraction . . . , I described
how Russian power inevitably poured into the vacuum left by the
destruction of power on its western frontier. The metaphoric image,
here, was seductive in its implication that politics obeys laws as
simple and absolute as those of classical physics. When we see what
actually happens in operational terms, however, in terms of armies
marching, statesmen negotiating, and people voting, the whole
situation appears to offer a range of possibilities incompatible with
the rigidity of physical laws. Accidents seem to play their part. The
mistakes of individual statesmen are seen to be significant. The
respiratory ailment that impaired Roosevelt's strength in the winter
of 1944–1945 has its effect. Unusual human weakness or unusual
human virtue appears to alter what might otherwise have been the
course of events. One hesitates to deny that Finland might have
gone the way that Czechoslovakia finally went. One hesitates to
affirm that Czechoslovakia never had the possibility of retaining
such freedom as Finland managed to retain.

We must beware of the absoluteness of the great abstractions
represented by the metaphor of the power vacuum. We must assume
a range of choice in the actual play of events. But the range may be
small at any one time (although cumulatively large over the genera-
tions), and so the metaphor may not be altogether misleading.

If one puts food before a sufficiently hungry child, warning it that
indigestion may be the consequence of eating it, our knowledge of
human nature makes it predictable that the child will end, after
whatever hesitation, by eating it nevertheless. Moscow, one sup-
poses, was not unmindful of future trouble in the prospect of

---

Mr. Halle is Professor of International Relations at the Institute for Advanced
International Studies in Geneva.

Abridgement of pp. 75, 76, 148, 153–160, 412–413 in *The Cold War As History* by
Louis J. Halle. Copyright © 1967 by Louis J. Halle. Reprinted by permission of
Harper & Row, Publishers, Inc.

swallowing the more-or-less indigestible nations that lay before it in Europe as the War ended. Therefore it maintained a considerable degree of self-restraint in its confrontation with Finland, of which it had already had some experience, and it showed some hesitation in confronting other possible victims. There was an initial reluctance over Poland, and an abstemiousness of some duration with respect to Czechoslovakia. In each particular instance, however, in which one has the power to dispose of a frightening enemy at the gate, and to replace him with a trusted servitor, a failure to exercise it must seem to be a folly by which one invites one's own destruction.

It is really not conceivable that the rulers in Moscow, with a thousand years of desperate struggle for survival behind them, would have abjured power-politics after the War and cooperated in the organization of a postwar world that represented the ideals of Anglo-Saxon political philosophy. This would have been for them to commit a kind of suicide, for it would have implied the dissolution of the secret and tyrannical regime on which they depended, inside Russia, for their own survival.

The range of choice, then, was small, the element of predetermination large. In the end Poland or Czechoslovakia might have retained a bit more freedom, Finland might have retained less. But this would not have represented a basically different situation. When the whole structure of power that had balanced and contained Russia on the west was shattered, then it was practically if not theoretically inevitable that the Russian power would expand. And so it did.

History is like a Shakespearian tragedy. Hamlet need not have suffered the fate that befell him—but only if he had not been Hamlet.

What we see throughout this history is the dynamism of the self-fulfilling prophecy. Moscow, anticipating a threat from the West, expands its empire in that direction, thereby provoking a reaction that confirms its anticipation. Washington, reacting in fear of Moscow's spreading tyranny, provokes the spread and intensification of that tyranny by moving to contain it, thereby confirming the fear on which it had acted. This is not to say that dangers can always be averted by not acting upon their anticipation. We face, here, a condition of "absolute predicament or irreducible dilemma."

The dialectic of conflict is in large measure unavoidable, although it can be mitigated by the manner in which it is conducted. It can be mitigated by a policy of speaking softly when one's own safety makes it necessary to show a big stick. This is where the practice of diplomacy as a peace-keeping art stands supreme. . . .

In politics, as in all human affairs, words are deeds. A declaration of war, for example, while it is merely a form of words, has the effect of a blow struck, and what follows is physical violence. An announcement by one side in a conflict that the other is about to start a war (which everyone must consequently prepare for) is bound to make the other apprehensive that the announcement is merely a prelude to the inauguration of a war by the side that made it. Alarmist language impells both sides to arm and prepare. On both sides, reasonableness and moderation are discredited; the representatives of extremism tend to achieve the seats of influence and power. Each side is impelled by its own fears to bemonster the other, cultivating the image of a ravening beast, called "the Enemy," that is bent on the enslavement of mankind. The situation is made to appear desperate, thereby justifying resort to measures of desperation. . . .

The tendency to go to linguistic extremes was certainly aggravated by the psychological dynamics that characterize all societies, and especially their bureaucracies, in wartime. Men who are rivaling one another for advancement in a governmental bureaucracy become involved in the competitive manifestation of zeal for the cause, the competitive demonstration of their identification with it. In the atmosphere of wartime they all feel themselves under observation and under suspicion of not being perfect in their appreciation of the evil that the enemy represents. So a rivalry in demonstrative extremism gets under way. The composition of the speeches that Zhdanov and Malenkov made at the Silesian conference may not have been uninfluenced by an awareness of Stalin's increasingly suspicious disposition. Those speeches, in turn, set a standard that the other members of the conference would try to equal or surpass. This kind of thing occurs in all societies and in all governments. In Washington after 1949 it would take the form of a shrill and fanatical anti-Communism, increasingly divorced from real circumstances, that would approach if not equal the extremes exemplified by the Communist world.

This dynamism of conflict would immediately engender, now, another element of the totality that I have identified with the Cold War. Each side would insist, and would in some measure convince itself, that the other aimed to make itself master of the whole world. (In the same way, during the two World Wars all good Americans and Englishmen knew that, in the first case the Kaiser, and in the second Hitler, was aiming at the conquest of the world.) Each, in attributing this unlimited objective to the other, would thereby be led to the conclusion that the struggle could be resolved only by the total defeat of the one side or the other—as in the wars between Rome and Carthage. Western politicians, paraphrasing Lincoln, would announce that the world could not exist half slave and half free (although it always had). Communist leaders, citing Marx, would proclaim the inevitable doom of the capitalist world, its total defeat and destruction (which Marx had expected to take place not later than the end of the nineteenth century). The objective, once again, could be nothing less than unconditional surrender.

The concept of total victory or total defeat as the only alternatives was bound to appeal especially to many American military men, whose professional training and indoctrination disposed them to accept, uncritically, the view to which General MacArthur would later give expression, that "in war there is no substitute for victory." At the council-tables of government and on private occasions they would begin to manifest an unhappy impatience with the policies of the civilians under whose orders, nevertheless, they would continue faithfully to serve. I have no doubt that there were circles in Moscow where a like attitude was manifested.

The Declaration adopted by the Silesian conference, in connection with the founding of the Cominform, represents the official view of the Cold War, henceforth binding on all Communist parties and their members. It states that:

> While the war was on, the Allied States in the war against Germany and Japan went together and comprised one camp. . . . [After the

war] two camps were formed—the imperialist and anti-democratic camp having as its basic aim the establishment of world domination of American imperialism and the smashing of democracy, and the anti-imperialist and democratic camp having as its basic aim the undermining of imperialism, the consolidation of democracy, and the eradication of the remnants of fascism. . . . The Truman–Marshall plan is only a constituent part, the European subsection of the general plan for the policy of global expansion pursued by the United States in all parts of the world. The plan for the economic and political enslavement of Europe by American imperialism is being supplemented by plans for the economic and political enslavement of China, Indonesia, the South American countries. . . . Under these circumstances it is necessary that the anti-imperialist democratic camp should close its ranks, draw up an agreed program of actions and work out its own tactics against the main forces of the imperialist camp, against American imperialism and its British and French allies. . . .

A resolution of the conference charged the newly instituted Cominform "with the organization of interchange of experience, and if need be, coordination of the activities of the Communist Parties on the basis of mutual agreement."

One of the Cominform's first undertakings was represented by the strikes and disorders that began in France and Italy in November. What their ultimate failure signified was the failure of Stalin's policy of pushing the West over the brink, on which it balanced, into economic disaster.

A few months later, on March 17, 1948, in a special Message to Congress, President Truman would say:

> Since the close of hostilities the Soviet Union and its agents have destroyed the independence and democratic character of a whole series of nations in Eastern and Central Europe. It is this ruthless course of action, and the clear design to extend it to the remaining free nations of Europe, that have brought about the critical situation in Europe today. . . . The Soviet Union and its satellites were invited to cooperate in the European Recovery Program. They rejected the invitation. More than that, they have declared their violent hostility to the program and are aggressively attempting to wreck it. They see in it a major obstacle to their designs to subjugate the free community of Europe. . . . I am sure that the determination of the free countries of

Europe to protect themselves will be matched by an equal determination on our part to help them do so.

The President would then ask Congress to enact legislation providing for universal military training and for the re-institution of conscription, which had been dropped at the end of the War.

On the same day that the President was to send this Message to Congress the foreign ministers of Great Britain, France, Belgium, Holland, and Luxembourg, would meet together in Brussels to sign a treaty providing for a collective defense in case of an armed attack on any one of them. The project of such a treaty, establishing what was called "Western Union," had first been advanced by British Foreign Minister Bevin in the House of Commons on January 22 as a response to the creation of the Cominform.

So we see how, by a self-perpetuating dialectic, a process of action and reaction back and forth between the two sides, the Cold War grew rapidly in magnitude and intensity. This process would continue—toward what end no one, at the time, could foretell.

In ideological terms, the Cold War presented itself as a worldwide contest between liberal democracy and Communism. Each side looked forward to the eventual supremacy of its system all over the earth. The official Communist goal was the liberation of mankind from capitalist oppression. Ideologically-minded Westerners interpreted this as signifying that Moscow was trying to impose its own authoritarian system on a world that it meant to rule. Americans, for their part, had traditionally looked forward to the liberation of mankind from the oppression of autocracy, and to the consequent establishment of their own liberal system throughout the world. To the ideologists in Moscow this meant that "the imperialist ruling circles" in America were trying to enslave all mankind under the yoke of Wall Street.

The ideological view of human affairs has always had an irresistible popular appeal because it conforms to the child's image of a world divided between two species, the good (we) and the wicked (they). According to this image, the essence of life is the struggle between good and evil so represented. The two contesting species take many different forms but are always essentially the same. On one occasion they may take the form of the cops and the robbers, on another that of the cowboys and the Indians, on another that of "peace-loving" and "aggressor" nations. In orthodox Marxism they take the form of the proletarians and the capitalists. This is the universal fairy-tale of mankind, to which we are all brought up. Any struggle cast in terms of it must properly be total. It would be improper for the cops to negotiate a compromise settlement with the robbers, or to limit the efforts they make to overcome them by such rules of combat as would be appropriate in a boxing-match, where the moral issue is absent. Christians in the Middle Ages were limited by explicit rules of chivalry and ecclesiastical law when they fought one another, but not when they fought pagans. When they fought pagans the only proper objective was that of eliminating them, or what they represented, from the face of the earth. Similarly, to the extent that the Cold War was to be regarded as an ideological contest there could be no geographical limitation to it, and it could properly end only when one side had, at last, destroyed the other.

The ideological view, however, is in its essence mythical. The grand eschatological objectives that go with it tend to have little or no expression beyond the nominal. They are not, in any case, objectives toward which the daily operations of government are actually directed. At no time, after the first years of the Bolshevik regime, was the operative policy of Moscow directed in any immediate or meaningful sense toward the objective of a single classless and stateless society encircling the globe. This was, rather, a nominal objective that pertained to a mythological future. As such, however, it had a noble simplicity that made it more real to the man in the street than such operative objectives as that of acquiring the "glacis" of secure territory along the western frontier of the traditional Russian state.

This is not to say that the ideology, with its grand objective, did not make a difference. It made a great difference. Not only did it constantly threaten to draw the makers of policy into foolish and dangerous adventures (for example, the 1920 march on Warsaw), it gave a mythic justification to the distrust of the outside world that, in fact, had other roots; it provided its votaries with a sense of mission; it furnished a cover of respectability for political practices that, in their nakedness, would have seemed shameful; it made those who were driven by terrible necessity to the perpetration of sinister deeds feel themselves morally justified. From the first, however, the deeds themselves were directed toward more limited and practical objectives that were not essentially different from the traditional objectives of the Russian state. While the nominal ideology had an influence that one could only regard as dangerous, what was determinative for action was the complex of considerations, representing power-politics, that stemmed from the self-interest of the Russian state.

President Wilson's objective of making the world "safe for democracy" had, in a detached view, implications not altogether unrelated to those arising from the ideological objectives associated with the Russian state since 1917. The influence of that abiding objective was, on occasion, dangerous—as in the ideological interventions that the United States undertook in Latin America immediately after World War II, as in its commitment to the maintenance of liberal democracy in China. In the long run, however, what was generally determinative for the operating policy of the United States, as for that of Soviet Russia, was its own vital interests in a world of power-politics.

In practice neither the United States nor the Soviet Union was bent on establishing its rule over the earth. Each, however, could be represented, with a certain show of plausibility, as seeking to do so. The Cold War would tend to be intractable and unlimitable to the extent that each side allowed itself to be entranced by the nominal and ideological questions at issue, subordinating the real, strategic questions.

All ideologically minded societies are given to a rhetoric of generalization that, in its literal application, is absolute and universal. This rhetoric may not be intended for such application in the practical world. The American founding fathers, for example, did not intend to apply the saying that all men are created equal to the status of Negro slaves in their society. Again, although the immediate situation that caused the United States to enter World War I was the torpedoing of merchant ships outside its Atlantic harbors by German submarines, which made the menace of German expansion seem vivid as never before, when the nation responded by going to war against Germany the nominal cause that it proclaimed was "freedom of the seas"—a formulation that did not distinguish the waters off its Atlantic harbors from the Sea of Okhotsk. Again, the purpose of the United States "to make the world safe for democracy" did not put Europe ahead of Asia or Africa. This rhetoric of World War I presented the American people with generalizations of local situations that led them to think in global terms, and that thereby strengthened the tendency of all war to overspread geographical and other limits.

The proclamation of the Truman Doctrine represents the same disposition. In 1947 it was the expansion of the Soviet Union in Europe only that had upset the balance of power and that represented a mortal danger to the Atlantic community of which the United States and Canada were the only undisabled members. The immediate danger was in Europe, not in the Pacific or South Asia or Africa. It was the situation in Europe that called for containment. Nevertheless, what the Truman Doctrine said was that "it must be the policy of the United States to support free peoples who are resisting attempted subjugation by armed minorities or by outside pressures." The concept this represented was simpler and grander than that of containing only Russia's expansion, and containing it from a particular point on the Baltic to a particular point on the Adriatic; but it was also less practicable. Taken literally, it covered the whole globe, applying to attempted subjugation of any free people anywhere by any armed minority or any outside pressure. So taken, it imposed an unlimited commitment on the United States, a commitment that might extend it far beyond its resources. Finally, it could only aggravate the fear of encirclement that had haunted Moscow for so many centuries. Who could say that it did not mean the use of the atomic bomb to enforce the American conception of freedom all around the globe? We Americans knew that we intended no such thing, but the Russians had a less benign picture of our character and our intentions.

We must distinguish, then, between the conflict represented by ideology and rhetoric, which was global and at best secondary, and the real conflict, which was over the balance of power that had its fulcrum in Europe. What the United States actually set out to do in 1947 was simply to defend what was left of Europe against an expanding Russia. If the resulting conflict was to spread to Asia, to

Africa, or to Latin America, that would be an unfortunate development of later days which the statesmanship of the time might well have been seeking to avert.

We may compare the Cold War, as we may the two World Wars that preceded it, to an earthquake, which occurs in a particular locality but sends its tremors all around the globe. . . .

All nations cultivate myths that endow them with dignity and, when occasion arises, give nobility to the causes in which they fight. A simple view would have it that myths, being fictional, must therefore be false. In a more sophisticated view, myths belong to the conceptual world by which, alone, we are able to interpret the existential world that constitutes our raw environment. This conceptual world, even if fictional, provides interpretations of the existential world that we must assume to be true in some degree. Most of us would agree that Shakespeare's *Hamlet* is a piece of fiction that represents truth in a high degree. Einstein's special theory of relativity is also a piece of fiction that, we suppose, represents truth in a high degree.

We men have to live, then, in two worlds at once, the conceptual and the existential, and our central problem is to maintain the correspondence between them. It is when these two worlds diverge excessively that we find ourselves in serious trouble.

Under circumstances of conflict between individuals or societies, and to the degree that conflict becomes passionate, the respective conceptual formulations of the parties tend to diverge from the existential realities they ostensibly represent. Fear, hatred, and the need for self-justification find their expression in conceptual falsification, whether innocent or deliberate.

Whenever an international conflict breaks out, each side is impelled to construct what we might call an advocate's account of the existential circumstances by which to identify itself with righteousness and its opponent with evil. At its crudest this takes the form of deliberately fabricated propaganda. More commonly it takes forms that are, at least in a subjective sense, less corrupt. When a people is called on by its national leadership to sacrifice all comfort and happiness for the sake of victory, the leadership is driven to create a mythology (in which it generally believes itself) that will serve to justify such sacrifices in their eyes. So it creates, for example, the myth of a proletarian struggle against wicked capitalists that is destined to bring about, at last, a classless society in which universal justice and happiness will be established forevermore; or it creates the myth of a worldwide contest between "peace-loving" and "aggressor" nations; and so the divergence between the existential and the conceptual is widened, with potentially tragic results. The false myth that inspires a people to fight successfully may obviate the possibility of crowning its success by the conclusion of a peace. . . .

II Dissenting Perspectives on the Crucial Issues

The following eight writers present a sharp dissent from the conventional viewpoint in a number of specific and crucial areas. As in the orthodox school, there are also important differences within the revisionist camp. Alperovitz stresses the primary role of the American atomic monopoly in precipitating a shift of policy after Roosevelt's death. Horowitz and Morray imply a calculated insensitivity to Soviet anxieties over international control of nuclear weapons. Paterson, on the other hand, emphasizes the importance of the United States' failure to grant Russia a loan in driving Stalin to a hardened cold war posture. Although stressing this particular economic policy rather than the bomb, he appears to agree with the other three writers on the proposition that the cold war would not have been inevitable if the United States had pursued different policies.

In their discussion of a third area of conflict, Eastern Europe, Williams and Kolko agree with Paterson on the significance of economic factors, but suggest that it was not so much a single action, but rather the broader context in which policy developed, which lay at the root of the problems of Soviet-American relations. Williams finds a long tradition in the United States of seeking to advance the national interest through the "open door" of economic penetration. Kolko, somewhat more deterministically, views American policy toward Eastern Europe as a relatively automatic function of a certain stage of capitalist development. Their arguments suggest the inevitability of the cold war. Viewing American policy in this area as a function of basic economic assumptions and structure, they infer, unlike the first four writers, that it really did not matter that much who was in the White House.

In his analysis of the Truman Doctrine, Fleming reverts to the idea that the cold war would by no means have been inevitable had

Truman continued Roosevelt's policies. He holds no single factor responsible for this fateful shift. The bomb, the economy, the emergence of a leadership more given to absolutist and militarist modes of thought and, especially, the activation of a latent anti-Soviet obsession going back to 1917—all, Fleming believes, played a role in Truman's policies.

Finally, Gardner attempts to show how George Kennan's containment theory filled a basic psychological and ideological need in the cold war mentality of certain circles in Washington and became, contrary to Kennan's original intention, a kind of *idée fixe* to be ritualistically chanted in justifying American policies from 1947 onward. He makes no specific judgment on the question of inevitability, although he stresses, as do Williams and Kolko (but with less economic emphasis), the continuity of American foreign policy assumptions in the years prior to 1947.

In contrast to the orthodox writers, these eight authors agree, despite their divergent analytical positions, that the United States must, on balance, bear a very substantial portion of the blame for originating the cold war.

GAR ALPEROVITZ
Atomic Diplomacy

THE MOST IMPORTANT point is the most general: Contrary to a commonly held view, it is abundantly clear that the atomic bomb profoundly influenced the way American policy makers viewed political problems. Or, as Admiral Leahy has neatly summarized the point, "One factor that was to change a lot of ideas, including my own, was the atom bomb . . . " The change caused by the new weapon was quite specific. It did not produce American opposition to Soviet policies in Eastern Europe and Manchuria. Rather, since a consensus had already been reached on the need to take a firm stand against the Soviet Union in both areas, the atomic bomb *confirmed* American leaders in their judgment that they had sufficient power to affect developments in the border regions of the Soviet Union. There is both truth and precision in Truman's statement to Stimson that the weapon "gave him an entirely new feeling of confidence."

This effect was a profoundly important one. Before the atomic bomb was tested, despite their desire to oppose Soviet policies, Western policy makers harbored very grave doubts that Britain and America could challenge Soviet predominance in Eastern Europe. Neither Roosevelt nor Truman could have confidence that the American public would permit the retention of large numbers of conventional troops in Europe after the war. (And Congressional rejection of Truman's military-training program later confirmed the pessimistic wartime predictions.) Thus, at the time of the Yalta Conference, as Assistant Secretary of State William L. Clayton advised Secretary Stettinius, "a large credit . . . appear[ed] to be the only concrete bargaining lever for use in connection with the many other political and economic problems which will arise between our two countries."

That this lever of diplomacy was not sufficiently powerful to force Soviet acceptance of American proposals was amply demonstrated

Mr. Alperovitz is a Fellow of the John F. Kennedy Institute of Politics at Harvard and of Kings College, Cambridge.

during the late-April and early-May crisis over Poland. Despite Truman's judgment that "the Russians needed us more than we needed them," Stalin did not yield to the firm approach. Hence, without the atomic bomb it seemed exceedingly doubtful that American policy makers would be able substantially to affect events within the Soviet-occupied zone of Europe. It may well be that, had there been no atomic bomb, Truman would have been forced to reconsider the basic direction of his policy as Churchill had done some months earlier. . . . It remained for Byrnes to summarize the early-1945 relative strengths of the powers: "It was not a question of what we would *let* the Russians do, but what we could *get* them to do."

As I have shown, this appraisal was radically changed by the summer of 1945. Since Byrnes advised Truman on both the atomic bomb and the need for strong opposition to the Russians in Eastern Europe before the President's first confrontation with Molotov, the new weapon's first impact possibly can be seen as early as the April showdown. However, no final judgment can be rendered on this point, using the evidence presently available. But there is no question that by the middle of July leading American policy makers were convinced that the atomic bomb would permit the United States to take a "firm" stand in subsequent negotiations. In fact, American leaders felt able to demand *more* at Potsdam than they had asked at Yalta. Again, Churchill's post-atomic appraisal is in striking contrast to his view of the pre-atomic realities: "We now had something in our hands which would redress the balance with the Russians." And Byrnes's new advice to Truman was quite straightforward: "The bomb might well put us in a position to dictate our own terms. . . . "

Once the profound impact of the atomic bomb upon American judgments is recognized, considerable light is cast upon the complicated events of the summer of 1945. The curious reversals in American Polish policy and the Hopkins mission both become understandable. The period is one in which two groups of officials debated strategy. Although there were differences of emphasis, since all agreed on the broad objective of attempting to force the Soviet Union into cooperative relationships in Eastern and Central Europe, the real struggle was over timing. Those outside the War

Department who had little knowledge or little faith in the as yet untested atomic weapon argued that an immediate showdown was necessary. In this their views paralleled Churchill's, who, having come to terms on the Balkans, feared a further weakening of Western determination, combined with a withdrawal of American troops, would convince Stalin time was on his side if he dug in while the West melted away.

Secretary Stimson, however, was able to counter this argument in two ways: He was able to show that conventional strength on the Continent would not be substantially reduced during the two months' delay until the atomic test; and he was able to promise that if a confrontation could be postponed the United States would soon be possessed of "decisive" powers. After forcing a premature showdown on the symbolic Polish issue, Truman reversed himself and accepted Stimson's broad strategy. The price he paid for delay was not high; he was forced to yield the substance of the point at issue in the Polish controversy, and he had to withdraw American troops to the agreed zonal positions in Germany. Significantly, he later characterized his first attempt to utilize economic bargaining strength through the Lend-Lease cutoff as a "mistake." From Truman's point of view, not only was the first showdown badly timed, but the need to reverse his public position and to send Hopkins on a mission of conciliation must have been a great personal embarrassment.

However, it is vital to recognize that Truman's conciliatory actions during late May, June, and early July did not represent his basic policy. He had demonstrated in the April showdown and in the decision to maintain American troop positions in Germany that his view of how to treat with Russia was far different from Roosevelt's. His decision abruptly to cut off Lend-Lease, his show of force over the Trieste dispute, his reconsideration of Roosevelt's Far Eastern agreement, his breach of the Balkans understandings, his refusal to adhere to the Yalta reparations accord—all these acts testify to the great gulf between his view and the view of his predecessor.

Those who argue that "Mr. Truman intended to continue the policy laid down by President Roosevelt" have focused attention on an extremely brief period when Truman did indeed adopt a more moderate approach. But his actions during this period—symbolized by his attempt to avoid the appearance of "ganging up" with Britain against the Soviet Union—were only a manifestation of his tactical retreat. In a fundamental sense, even the conciliatory period can only be explained by recognizing that its primary purpose was not to continue Roosevelt's policy, but to facilitate a far different policy based upon the overwhelming power soon to be available. Truman replaced the symbolic April showdown over Poland with a parallel August and September effort in the Balkans. Both before and after the brief conciliatory period, the President's attitude is best summed up in the statement he made eight days after Roosevelt's death: He "intended to be firm with the Russians and make no concessions." And both before and after the temporary period of no "ganging up," Truman's effort to coordinate policy with Britain was a hallmark of his approach. As Byrnes has written, Molotov's conclusion that American policy had changed after Roosevelt's death was "understandable."

The Potsdam meeting clearly illustrates how the strategic decision to wait for the atomic bomb dominated American policy making from mid-May until early August. The primary reason most Western leaders began to call for another meeting with Stalin only three months after Yalta was their desire to have a confrontation on the important European questions then in tense dispute. But, . . . Truman rejected the advice of his advisers and Churchill, and twice postponed a face-to-face meeting with Stalin because of his decision to wait for the atomic bomb. Ironically, however, in the end he committed himself to a meeting which was still a scant two weeks too early to be decisive. For this reason, to focus attention on the Potsdam meeting itself, as many writers have done, is to completely misunderstand American policy. Indeed, the interesting question is not what happened at the meeting, but why very little happened at all.

Thus, the importance of the atomic bomb in American calculations is underscored by the negative result of the heads-of-government meeting: had the new weapon not played such a crucial role in American strategy, there would have been every reason for Truman to attempt to achieve a negotiated settlement as quickly as possible after the defeat of Germany. Assuming, as Churchill did until mid-July, that it was unwise to gamble on the possibilities of the as yet untested weapon, the Prime Minister was undoubtedly correct to argue that "the decisive, practical points of strategy" involved "*above all,* that a settlement must be reached on all major issues between the West and the East . . . *before the armies of democracy melted . . .* " As he told Eden, the "issue . . . seems to me to dwarf all others." Without the atomic bomb, Churchill believed, the only hope lay in an "early and speedy showdown." . . .

. . . Once the detailed report of the atomic test arrived at Potsdam, Churchill reversed himself completely: "We were . . . possessed of powers which were irresistible." But Churchill's pre-Potsdam appraisal of Stalin's position was probably correct; for, unless the West was prepared to negotiate a settlement, the Soviet Premier undoubtedly calculated there was everything to gain if he waited until the American troops were withdrawn from the Continent. Since Truman did not tell Stalin of the atomic bomb, it could not yet be expected to play a major role in Soviet-American relations. And, indeed, with no apparent changes in the power relationships, on most issues discussed at the Conference, *both* Truman and Stalin held their ground. The Potsdam Conference took place at a unique moment in history, when each side undoubtedly believed time was on its side. The logic of the situation ensured—as the final protocol showed—that the Conference could only end in deadlock. . . .

He [Truman] believed that the United States had sufficient power to force Soviet acceptance of the American plan for lasting world peace. Above all, his policy required a stable Europe based upon democratic governments and a sound Continental economy. There were two fundamental reasons why the President believed the atomic bomb would permit him to implement his plan: On the one hand, after a new symbolic showdown, the bomb seemed likely to force Soviet agreement to American economic and political plans for Eastern Europe; and, on the other, its power meant that there was no need to fear another German revival—the German economic contribution to Continental stability could be given priority over industrial disarmament schemes.

Truman's own argument that a stable Europe was vital to world peace and to American security reveals the error of the common opinion that America had little active interest in European affairs until the 1947 Truman Doctrine and Marshall Plan. The President's mid-1945 declaration to his staff was an accurate statement of American policy: "We were committed to the rehabilitation of Europe, and there was to be no abandonment this time." Indeed, much more must be said, for the American commitment to Europe was not restricted to the Western regions of the Continent. As George F. Kennan, the author of the "containment policy," has emphasized, American policy was "by no means limited to holding the line." And as Byrnes has repeatedly stressed, in 1945 and 1946 senior American officials were not primarily concerned with a Soviet political or military threat to Western Europe; their eyes were focused on conditions in the Soviet-occupied zone. Byrnes has been quite explicit; his policy always aimed at forcing the Russians to yield in Eastern Europe, and in mid-1947 he still continued to argue that the United States had it in its power to force the Russians to "retire in a very decent manner."

There is no question that Byrnes's policy derived from the best intentions and the highest ideals. And there is no reason to doubt Truman's statement that "the one purpose which dominated me in everything I thought and did was to prevent a third world war." Nevertheless, the attempt to force Soviet withdrawal from Eastern Europe immediately after Hitler's invasion of Russia was an extremely difficult policy to implement. And, inevitably, the policy's problems were greatly multiplied when doubts were raised as to whether or not the industrial basis of German power would be weakened as had been agreed. It may well be true, as Walter Lippmann observed at the time, "that the best that was possible [was] an accommodation, a *modus vivendi,* a working arrangement, some simple form of cooperation, and that in demanding more than that we have been getting less than that, making the best the enemy of the good."

Secretary Stimson seems to have shared this judgment and also to have recognized that the atomic bomb compounded the difficulties Truman's idealistic policy faced. By early September the Secretary of War had come full circle, concluding that "I was wrong" and that the attempt to use the atomic bomb to gain diplomatic objectives was "by far the more dangerous course." In a profoundly ironic, but unsuccessful, attempt to change the policy he had launched, shortly before leaving office Stimson urged an immediate and direct approach to Moscow to attempt to establish international control of atomic energy which might head off "an armament race of a rather desperate character." Apparently greatly disturbed by the bombing of Hiroshima, and now openly opposed to Secretary Byrnes, he advised: *"If we fail to approach them now and merely continue to negotiate with them, having this weapon rather ostentatiously on our hip, their suspicions and their distrust of our purposes and motives will increase."*

At the same time Stimson offered this advice, Secretary Byrnes attempted to explain to Molotov that the United States was "not interested in seeing anything but governments friendly to the Soviet Union in adjacent countries." But the Soviet Foreign Minister was openly incredulous: "I must tell you I have doubts as to this, and it would not be honest to hide it." Similarly, at this time former Soviet Foreign Minister Litvinov asked an American friend: "Why did you Americans wait till right now to begin opposing us in the Balkans and Eastern Europe? You should have done this three years ago. Now it is too late, and your complaints only arouse suspicions here." And General Eisenhower, making a triumphal postwar visit to Moscow, sensed new and profound Soviet suspicions: "Before the atom bomb was used I would have said, yes, I was sure we could keep the peace with Russia. Now I don't know. . . . People are frightened and disturbed all over. Every one feels insecure again."

To recall the judgments of Stimson and Eisenhower in the autumn of 1945 is to state the ultimate question of to what extent the atomic bomb affected the entire structure of postwar American-Soviet relations. But it is not possible at this juncture to test Secretary Stimson's September view that "the problem of our satisfactory relations with Russia [was] not merely connected with but [was] virtually dominated by the problem of the atomic bomb." Nor can the issue of why the atomic bomb was used be conclusively resolved. . . .

At present no final conclusion can be reached on this question. But the problem can be defined with some precision: Why did the American government refuse to attempt to exploit Japanese efforts to surrender? Or, alternatively, why did they refuse to test whether a Russian declaration of war would force capitulation? Were Hiroshima and Nagasaki bombed primarily to impress the world with the need to accept America's plan for a stable and lasting peace—that is, primarily, America's plan for Europe? The evidence strongly suggests that the view which the President's personal representative offered to one of the atomic scientists in May 1945 was an accurate statement of policy: "Mr. Byrnes did not argue that it was necessary to use the bomb against the cities of Japan in order to win the war . . . Mr. Byrnes's . . . view [was] that our possessing and demonstrating the bomb would make Russia more manageable in Europe. . . . "

DAVID HOROWITZ
Free World Colossus

THE EARLY APPROACHES to the control of atomic energy reveal a . . . pattern in the strategy of US leaders in this period. Indeed just as there were two divergent views on the problem of Europe, so there was a wide split in high policy circles on how to come to grips with the Atomic question. Moreover, the basis for this split also rested squarely on an assessment of the Soviet future.

On September 11, 1945, Henry L. Stimson, retiring Secretary of War (and former Secretary of State under Hoover), sent a memorandum to President Truman on proposed action for control of the Atomic Bomb. Stimson's proposals were discussed at a crucial cabinet meeting ten days later. As the memorandum is a primary document in the sources of the cold war, it deserves to be considered at length.

The introduction of the Atomic Bomb, wrote Stimson, "has profoundly affected political considerations in all sections of the globe. In many quarters it has been interpreted as a substantial offset to the growth of Russian influence on the continent." The Soviet Government would be certain to have sensed this tendency, and "the temptation will be strong for the Soviet political and military leaders to acquire this weapon in the shortest possible time."

Britain, Stimson noted, had already in effect acquired the status of a "partner," with the United States, in the development of the weapon. "Accordingly, unless the Soviets are voluntarily invited into the partnership upon a basis of cooperation and trust, we are going to maintain the Anglo-Saxon bloc over against the Soviet in the possession of this weapon." Such a condition, Stimson concluded, would almost certainly stimulate "feverish" activity on the part of the Soviet Union toward the development of the bomb. This would mean "a secret armament race of a rather desperate charac-

Mr. Horowitz is editor of *Ramparts* Magazine.

ter." There was evidence, he added, "that such activity may have already commenced."

Whether Russia got control of the bomb in four years or a maximum of twenty, Stimson argued, was not as important as to make sure that when she got it, she was a willing and cooperative partner among the peace-loving nations of the world. "To put the matter concisely," he wrote, "*I consider the problem of our satisfactory relations with Russia as not merely connected with but as virtually dominated by the problems of the atomic bomb.*" Except for these problems, relations with Russia, while vitally important, might not be pressing. But with the discovery of the bomb, they have become "immediately emergent." [Emphasis added.]

"*Those relations,*" he stressed, "*may be perhaps irretrievably embittered by the way in which we approach the solution of the bomb with Russia. For if we fail to approach them now and merely continue to negotiate with them having this weapon rather ostentatiously on our hip, their suspicions and their distrust of our purposes and motives will increase.*" [Emphasis in original.]

A failure to approach Russia in such a way as to inspire her confidence would stimulate her to greater efforts in an all-out effort to solve the problem of the bomb. If a solution were achieved in that spirit, "it is much less likely that we will ever get the kind of covenant we may desperately need in the future."

Stimson therefore proposed that a direct approach be made to Russia by the United States. He was careful to underline his opinion that it must not appear as an Anglo-American gesture, which the Russians would be sure to distrust, nor as an action of any international group of nations, which would not be taken seriously by the Kremlin. "I emphasize *perhaps beyond all other considerations,*" he wrote, "the importance of taking this action with Russia as a proposal of the United States." [Emphasis added.]

Stimson's idea of an approach to Russia was to make a direct proposal to the effect that the United States would be prepared "to enter an arrangement with the Russians, the general purpose of which would be to control and limit the use of the atomic bomb as an instrument of war and so far as possible to direct and encourage the development of atomic power for peaceful and humanitarian purposes."

In the light of what actually became the American course in the early negotiations over atomic control, the concrete steps which Stimson suggested to implement his approach assume a special importance. "Such an approach [he wrote] might more specifically lead to the proposal that we would stop work on the further improvement in, or manufacture of, the bomb as a military weapon, provided the Russians and the British would agree to do likewise. It might also provide that we would be willing to impound what bombs we now have in the United States provided the Russians and the British would agree with us that in no event will they or we use a bomb as an instrument of war unless all three governments agree to that use."

In other words, under Stimson's plan, the United States would have agreed to yield its temporary military advantage, as a step towards proving its good faith as the more powerful of the two participants and the one that had actually used the bomb in a military operation. In return, the initial steps would have been taken to create a framework for cooperation in the development and control of atomic energy. The loss to the United States of a temporary military advantage would have been amply compensated by the great gain for humanity and ultimately for the United States as well. "Our objective," wrote Stimson, "must be to get the best kind of international bargain we can—one that has some chance of being kept and saving civilization not for five or twenty years, but forever." If the arrangement he outlined could be initiated, thought Stimson, the chances for real control would be much greater "than . . . if the approach were made as a part of a general international scheme or if the approach were made after a succession of express or implied threats or near threats in our peace negotiations."

Both the wisdom of these proposals and their practicality were appreciated by the majority of those present at the September 21 cabinet meeting. Seven cabinet members, including Dean Acheson, agreed with Stimson's appraisal and approach; Forrestal, Fred Vinson and Tom Clark were opposed, and two members wished to defer the decision until a later time. *Yet, in every subsequent step taken by the Truman Administration on this vital question, Stimson's major recommendations were not only disregarded but actually reversed.*

Above all else, Stimson had recommended that the approach to Russia on the atomic energy question to be an initiative of the United States alone, neither an Anglo-American proposal nor an action of any international group of nations. On November 15, scarcely two months after Stimson's strong admonitions against giving Russia the impression that the Anglo-Saxon bloc was to be maintained against her, the President of the United States, the Prime Minister of The United Kingdom (Attlee) and the Prime Minister of Canada (King) issued a joint statement calling for the establishment of a United Nations Commission for the control of atomic energy. They declared: "We desire that there should be full and effective cooperation in the field of atomic energy between the United States, the United Kingdom and Canada." And four months later, Truman sat on the platform at Fulton Missouri, while Churchill called for an Anglo-Saxon alliance against Soviet Russia.

Stimson's warning against making implied threats during the approach to the Soviet Union over the question of atomic controls, as well as his specific injunction against negotiating with the bomb "rather ostentatiously on our hip" were also completely ignored. Indeed, as with the previous initiative, to say merely that they were ignored is something of an understatement. The United States presented its first plan for the control of atomic energy to the United Nations on June 14, 1946, while the Soviet Union submitted its own proposals four days later. *Then, on July 1, with the discussions still in progress, the United States exploded an atomic bomb at Bikini as its first post-war atomic test. Pravda* immediately charged that the United States was trying to influence the talks (i.e. by "implied threat" exactly as Stimson had warned) and that the tests showed that the United States was not aiming at the restriction of atomic weapons, but at their perfection.

JOSEPH P. MORRAY
From Yalta to Disarmament

AT THE HEART of the Baruch Plan lay an ambition to effect a change in the international order over the expected opposition of the Soviet Union by exploiting the threat of the new weapons. Evidence of this purpose may be seen in the fact that the United States neglected to consult with the Soviet Union about the plan before presenting it publicly to the United Nations Commission. More evidence may be found in Mr. Baruch's disparagements of "mouthings about narrow sovereignty" and his advocacy of a new "international law with teeth in it" as security against war. Also, Dr. J. Robert Oppenheimer, who was a member of the board of consultants responsible for preparing the plan, wrote in the January 1948 issue of *Foreign Affairs:*

> Thus the problem as it appeared in the summer of 1945 was to use an understanding of atomic energy and the developments that we have carried out, with their implied hope and implied threat, to see whether in this area international barriers might not be broken down and patterns of candor and cooperation established which would make the peace of the world. . . .
>
> The prevalent view . . . saw in the problems of atomic energy . . . an opportunity to cause a decisive change in the whole trend of Soviet policy.

The Baruch Plan was hailed by most delegates on the Atomic Energy Commission as a forward-looking proposal, as indeed it was from the point of view of those who wanted to abolish the independence of the Soviet Union by bringing it under the control of a reliable new international authority. The plan was an "advance" on the outmoded sovereign equality of the great powers by reducing their number. Through the progressive principle of majority rule among diplomats the Soviet Union was to be tamed and neutralized. The United States, with admirable vision, conscience and courage, magnanimously consented to respect the decisions of an anti-

Mr. Morray is an Oregon attorney and writer on political affairs.

Reprinted by permission of Monthly Review Press. Copyright © 1961 by J. P. Morray.

Communist majority, providing the Soviet Union did the same. All the Soviet Union need do in order to share the joy of the majority at the prospect of the new order in international affairs was to abandon Communism in a sporting acknowledgment that God had willed to give the United States the first atomic bomb.

The threat of war was indeed to be reduced. This was no idle claim by the proponents of the Baruch Plan. It was to be reduced by freezing one of the antagonists into permanent, safeguarded subordination. When two rivals threaten to fight, the danger is reduced if one succeeds in establishing his right to be law-giver, judge, and policeman to the other.

In this sense the Baruch Plan was a grand design for peace. It was fashioned to fulfill President Truman's proclaimed purpose of making atomic energy "a powerful and forceful influence towards the maintanance of world peace." This peace could now be stabilized without any need for accommodation, which had been necessary at Yalta, to the views of the U.S.S.R. The monopoly of the bomb gave to the United States government for the moment a unique sense of security, darkened by the gloomy realization that the Soviet Union would sooner or later develop the bomb for itself. The Acheson-Lilienthal Report estimated, recognizing some "valid differences of opinion," that "during the next five to twenty years the situation will have changed profoundly." The plan proposed to use these intervening years in such a way as to perpetuate American security through an international authority framed to subdue Communist troublemakers. The plan proposed to exchange the security of the United States bomb monopoly for the security of a well-armed friendly policeman fully sharing United States views on the Communists. Before the reader condemns the Soviet Union for declining to ratify this design, let him imagine the relative position of the two states to be reversed and let him answer whether he would favor American acceptance of such an unprotected minority status in a Communist-dominated system.

Reservations in the plan as to relinquishing the bomb and sharing with the Authority information about the production of atomic energy gave further evidence of the important part played by the monopoly of the bomb in the revised American policy toward the Soviet Union. These two trumps were not to be released until the new system was fully operative to the satisfaction of the United States. These preconditions were stated by Mr. Baruch in the following words:

> When an adequate system for control of atomic energy, including the renunciation of the bomb as a weapon, has been agreed upon and put *into effective operation and condign punishments set up* for violations of the rules of control which are to be stigmatized as international crimes, we propose that
> 1. Manufacture of atomic bombs shall stop;
> 2. Existing bombs shall be disposed of *pursuant to the terms of the treaty,* and
> 3. The Authority shall be in possession of full information as to the know-how for the production of atomic energy.
> Let me repeat, so as to avoid misunderstanding: my country is ready to make its full contribution toward the end we seek, *subject of course to our constitutional processes, and to an adequate system of control becoming fully effective,* as we finally work it out. [*Italics added.*]

We have already noticed what the phrase "an adequate system of control" meant to the American government. It meant an actual monopoly by the Authority of all atomic energy activities, either directly through management or indirectly through licensing and supervision. Only when this had been put into "effective operation" would the United States let go of its advantage. Who was to judge when the operation was "effective"? The failure to designate any referee for this determination suggests that the United States intended to decide the question for itself. Henry Wallace, who was then Secretary of Commerce and presumably informed on American policy, confirmed that this was the purport of the American plan in a letter of July 23, 1946, to President Truman discussing the trend of American-Soviet relations. He criticized the American plan for "a fatal defect":

> That defect is the scheme . . . of requiring other nations to enter into binding commitments not to conduct research into the military uses of atomic energy and to disclose their uranium and thorium resources, while the United States retains the right to withhold its technical knowledge of atomic energy until the international control and inspection system is working to our satisfaction.

In other words, we are telling the Russians that if they are "good boys" we may eventually turn over our knowledge of atomic energy to them and to the other nations. But there is no objective standard of what will qualify them as being "good" nor any specified time for sharing our knowledge.

Mr. Baruch's answer to this was evasive:

> *It has always been recognized* that the precise content, sequence and timing of the transition stages would be the subject of *detailed negotiation* since the process of transition involves a shift from the present position of the United States [*from the pinnacle of power. JPM*] to a position of equality in the field of atomic energy among all nations participating in the plan. [*Italics added.*]

The promised memorandum on the content and sequence of transition stages was never forthcoming, presumably because the "appropriate time" never arrived. The United Nations Atomic Energy Commission functioned for three and one half years, and in three reports, approved by the majority over the opposition of the two Soviet-bloc members, developed in great detail the control aspects of the Baruch Plan, which had become "the majority plan." But there was never an "appropriate time" to say precisely when the United States would relinquish the bomb or share information on atomic energy production.

Mr. Baruch had also qualified the guarantee of United States readiness "to make its full contribution to the end we seek" with the phrase "subject, of course, to our constitutional processes." It is therefore necessary to look at what rights Congress was reserving to itself connected with the question of yielding useful information.

Concurrently with the preparation of the Acheson-Lilienthal Report and the Baruch Plan, Congress was drafting the Atomic Energy Act of 1946, which President Truman signed into law on August 1, 1946. By this law a United States Atomic Energy Commission was established for the domestic control of atomic energy. Congress considered the question of information control to have two aspects. American scientists stood to benefit from information received from foreigners, as the Manhattan Project had demonstrated. Yet to help other nations build atomic weapons or power plants would be against United States interests in the situation of 1946. . . .

Congress solved this dilemma by authorizing exchange of the types of information in which foreigners were traditionally ahead of Americans—the basic scientific and technical categories—and forbidding an exchange of those types—industrial know-how and military uses—in which Americans were sure to be well ahead. This must be called a realistic rather than a magnanimous solution. Section 10 (a) of the Act provides:

> (1) That *until Congress declares by joint resolution that effective and enforceable international safeguards* against the use of atomic energy for destructive purposes have been established, there shall be *no exchange of information with other nations with respect to the use of atomic energy for industrial purposes;* and
>
> (2) That the dissemination of scientific and technical information relating to atomic energy should be permitted and encouraged so as to provide that free interchange of ideas and criticisms which is essential to scientific progress. [*Italics added.*]

Thus Congress made clear, with the President's approval, that the determination of the effectiveness of international controls was one on which Congress reserved a veto for itself, whatever an international control body might declare on the issue. . . .

Further evidence that the United States was negotiating from the bomb is found in the letter to the Secretary of State transmitting the Acheson-Lilienthal Report, signed by Dean Acheson, Under-Secretary of State, chairman, and the other members of the special committee. This letter made clear that no recommendation was being made for the United States to give up the bomb at any particular time, though there was set forth an elaborate management and control system leading to the consolidation of the international Authority's monopoly of the atomic energy field. . . .

The committee, assigned the task of drafting terms for the outlaw's surrender to the forces of order, was not so presumptuous as to advise the vigilantes when to lay down their own weapons. Asking the United States government to wean itself from the bomb at any specific time was sure to provoke a storm of opposition, because where your treasure is there is your heart also. But avoiding the problem was tantamount to proposing an endless postponement. Dr. Oppenheimer, who gained his insights into realities as a member of the board of consultants, came to regard American addiction to the bomb as one of the major obstacles to international control. Writing in 1948 on the reasons for the collapse of the United Nations negotiations, he stated:

> There appears to be little doubt that at the present time our unique possession of the facilities and weapons of atomic energy constitute *military advantages which we only reluctantly would lay down.* There appears to be little doubt that we *yearn for the notion of a trusteeship* more or less as it was formulated by President Truman in his Navy Day Address of late 1945: we should desire, that is, a situation in which our pacific intent was recognized and in which the nations of the world would gladly *see us the sole possessors of atomic weapons.* As a corollary, we are reluctant to see any of the knowledge on which our present mastery of atomic energy rests, revealed to potential enemies. Natural and inevitable as these desires are, they nevertheless stand in bleak contradiction to our central proposals for the renunciation of sovereignty, secrecy and rivalry in the field of atomic energy. [*Italics added.*]

The American public would have been spared some vain hope and bitterness had the government proceeded to negotiate the question of atomic energy control privately with the Soviet Union before airing the Baruch Plan publicly in the United Nations Atomic Energy Commission. The Soviet leaders were bound to need time to consider carefully the effects of such radical proposals. It would have been a token of friendly relations and good will to give them a preview and an opportunity to share in the development of the plan. The precipitate resort to forensic tactics and the imperative tone of Mr. Baruch's words, sounding in fact like an ultimatum, were departures from the spirit of the wartime alliance and from the unanimity principle on which the United Nations had been founded. Such an approach cast doubt on the realism or on the good faith of the American leaders. Either the intoxication of self-confidence induced by the bomb gave rise to a dream that the U.S.S.R. could be hustled into a disadvantageous arrangement, or the government never really made a serious effort, despite the fanfare, to solve the problem of saving the human race from nuclear horror. . . .

Before examining the Soviet proposal and the Western response to it, let us continue to focus for the moment on the Baruch Plan and, in particular, on the reaction it evoked from the Soviet representatives. They attacked it at five points: (1) the scope of controls, (2) stages and timing of controls, (3) retention of the bomb by the United States during the transition period, (4) the manner of judging violations and imposing sanctions, and (5) the ultimate disposition of the weapons. These issues stand out from the turbulent flow of words evoked by Mr. Baruch's speech of June 14, 1946, and by the three reports of the Atomic Energy Commission to the Security Council and the General Assembly.

The U.S.S.R. attacked the Baruch control system of ownership, management and licensing as preparation for intrusion into the internal economies of all states by an American-dominated agency obedient to the interests of American capitalists. A few excerpts from the debates will illustrate the Soviet mode of attack. Speaking before the General Assembly on October 29, 1946, Mr. Molotov, Soviet Foreign Minister, discussed the Baruch Plan in these words:

> The United States plan, the so-called "Baruch plan," unfortunately suffers from a certain amount of egoism. It proceeds from the desire to secure for the United States of America the monopolistic posses-sion of the atomic bomb. At the same time, it calls for the earliest possible establishment of control over the production of atomic energy in all countries, giving to this control an international character in outward appearance, but in fact attempting to protect, in a veiled form, the monopolistic position of the United States in this field. It is obvious that projects of this kind are unacceptable, since they are based on a narrow conception of the interests of one country and on the inadmissible negation of the equal rights of states and of their legitimate interests. . . .

Judged against the standard of security adopted by the Baruch Plan, there could be no denial that the Soviet control plan was deficient. Assuming the existence of a will to manufacture weapons secretly, periodic inspection did not offer positive guarantees against diversion of nuclear materials. Nor did provision for special investigations on suspicion of clandestine activities make it certain that timely suspicions would arise to spring a special investigation before treachery had put together a supply of bombs. No Soviet answer could negate these dangers.

Nevertheless, the choice facing the Western powers was not between the Baruch Plan and the Soviet Plan. For good reasons implying no sinister intent the Baruch Plan was unacceptable to the Soviet Union. (It is also questionable whether the more remote stages would ever have been acceptable to the United States Congress.) The Baruch Plan was misguided because it failed to take account of Soviet determination to remain independent, at whatever risk, of Western domination. The Soviet Union did not want security at the price of the Baruch Plan. This was one of the conditions of the problem of international control. We cannot blame the Soviet leaders for cherishing their independence, for their "mouthings about narrow sovereignty." We must blame the American leaders for failing, or refusing, to look at the problem from the Soviet point of view. The United States had the initiative. It should have been used to diminish the peril of nuclear warfare, not to attempt with the threat of bombs to arrest the spread of Communism. The Baruch Plan, primarily an anti-Communist rather than an antinuclear design, was incongruous as a basis for negotiations with the Soviet Union.

The true choice facing American statesmen in 1946 and 1947 was between no agreement and some modification of the Soviet proposal. The Soviets had an acknowledged right to veto the Baruch Plan, and from the Communist point of view they were wise to do so. The United States also had an acknowledged right to veto the Soviet plan. When great powers negotiate, neither can dictate to the other. But for agreement there must be common ground; this means that each power must examine every proposal to see if it describes common ground. The Baruch proposal did not do so. This was doubtless a disappointment, but it was a fact.

Did the Soviet proposal describe common ground? Was the United States prepared to accept modest controls on its own atomic operations? On the record the answer seems to be, "Yes indeed! And more too!" Was the United States prepared to forego use and possession of the bomb? On the record this was a stage of its own proposal. The issue over international control of atomic energy finally has to be phrased: Were not the risks to mankind of nuclear catastrophe less under the Soviet Plan than under no agreement at all? Answers to that question will vary according to one's assessment of Communist techniques. Those who see the Communists as intending, when the time is ripe, to launch an all-out military attack on the remaining capitalist countries, will find the greatest of all risks in the possibility of a clandestine manufacture of nuclear weapons by a treacherous Soviet bloc. The number of those who attribute this plan to the Communists is steadily diminishing. If the reader finds himself among those who put a Soviet surprise nuclear attack as one of the less likely causes of the next world war, he may well conclude that the Soviet Plan, despite its authorship, should have been accepted as a basis for negotiations.

But that was not our destiny. Secretary of State Marshall in a speech to the General Assembly on September 17, 1947, reacted to the absolute Soviet rejection of the Baruch Plan with a hint that the discussions had failed of their purpose:

> If the minority persists in refusing to join with the majority, the Atomic Energy Commission may soon be faced with the conclusion that it is unable to complete the task assigned it.

The Assembly, however, wanted more perseverance from the commission, recalling perhaps Mr. Baruch's ominous words of the previous year that the world faced a choice "between the quick and the dead." The Soviet Union found support in resisting a move in 1948 to liquidate the commission, and the United States did not press its unpopular initiative. The talks dragged on with perfunctory repetitions of the familiar themes until January 1950, when the Soviet delegate stopped attending in protest against the continued presence of the representative of Nationalist China. This provided the awaited occasion for burying the commission, and all delegates turned gratefully to other tasks.

THOMAS G. PATERSON
The Abortive American Loan to Russia

THE AMERICAN AMBASSADOR to Moscow, W. Averell Harriman, cabled the Department of State in January 1945 that the Soviet Union placed "high importance on a large postwar credit as a basis for the development of 'Soviet-American relations.' From his [V. M. Molotov's] statement I sensed an implication that the development of our friendly relations would depend upon a generous credit." In October 1945, a diplomat at the Foreign Ministers Council meeting in London noted the issues which he thought were impeding amicable Russian-American relations—the atomic bomb and an American loan to Russia. A few years later, an associate of Donald M. Nelson, War Production Board chairman, wrote: "Although little publicized, the possibility of this loan for a time almost certainly influenced Soviet policy toward the United States, and its refusal coincided significantly with the increasing aggressiveness of the Kremlin."

In the 1943-1945 period, a postwar American loan to the Soviet Union might have served as peacemaker; but by the early part of 1946 both nations had become increasingly uncompromising on the major international issues, and the usefulness of a loan to the United States, to Russia, and to amicable and productive relations had been called into serious doubt. "Whether such a loan," Secretary of State Edward R. Stettinius, Jr., later wrote, "would have made the Soviet Union a more reasonable and cooperative nation in the postwar world will be one of the great 'if' questions of history." The recent availability of historical sources provides material for a suggestive answer to Stettinius' question. The evidence suggests that America's refusal to aid Russia through a loan similar to that granted to the British in early 1946, perhaps contributed to a continuation of a low standard of living for the Russian people with detrimental interna-

Mr. Paterson is Associate Professor of History at the University of Connecticut.

Thomas G. Paterson, "The Abortive American Loan to Russia and the Origins of the Cold War, 1943–1946," *Journal of American History*, LVI (June, 1969), pp. 70–92. Excerpted by permission of the Organization of American Historians and Thomas G. Paterson.

tional effects, to a less conciliatory and harsher Russian policy toward Germany and Eastern Europe, and to unsettled and inimical postwar Soviet-American relations.

World War II had been cruel to the Soviet Union. Coupled with the deaths of millions was the devastation of most of Western Russia. Over 30,000 industrial factories and 40,000 miles of railroad line had been destroyed. In 1945, Soviet agricultural output was about half the 1940 level. One state department study reported that the Soviet Union had lost sixteen billion dollars in fixed capital, or one quarter of the prewar total. Secretary of War Henry L. Stimson recorded that the "completeness of the destruction was absolute" in the Ukraine. To help repair the massive war damage, the Russians looked eagerly to the United States.

Shortly after his arrival in Moscow in October 1943, Harriman asked to meet with A. I. Mikoyan, the commissar for foreign trade, to discuss postwar American aid for Russian reconstruction. Harriman found the Russians "intensely interested." He indicated to Mikoyan that healthy postwar Russian-American trade financed by credits "would be in the self-interest of the United States to be able to afford full employment during the period of transition from war-time to peace-time economy." About the same time, Nelson, visiting with Premier Joseph Stalin in Moscow, told the Russian dictator that the United States had a "great surplus capacity for producing the goods that you need. We can find a way to do business together." . . .

In late January 1944, Mikoyan asked Harriman how large a postwar loan the Soviet Union could expect from the United States. Harriman, lacking specific instructions, could not answer. On February 1, Mikoyan suggested a figure of one billion dollars to run for twenty-five years with .5 percent interest. Harriman demurred; he found the amount too large, the repayment schedule too liberal, and the interest rate too low. The state department still had no clear policy on a Russian loan and urged Harriman to "limit yourself to generalities" because Washington was worried about "certain legal limitations."

Harriman, eager to proceed in order to exercise diplomatic leverage on the Russians, was unhappy with American lethargy in early 1944. . . . The United States should move with haste to secure an agreement with Russia on reconstruction assistance for three reasons. First, he noted its value to the American economy "in cushioning the shock from war to peace if we are prepared to put into production Russian orders immediately upon cessation of hostilities." Second, an agreement would spur the Russian war effort. And, finally (Harriman revealed the uses to which the United States would put its postwar economic power):

> . . . if aid for reconstruction is to be of real value in our over-all relations with the Soviets as a benefit which can be obtained from us if they work cooperatively with us on international problems *in accordance with our standards,* we must have a well forged instrument to offer them. Vague promises excite Soviet suspicions whereas a precise program offered to them (but always kept within our control thru the approval of each transaction) will, in my judgement, be of definite value.

. . .

On January 3, 1945, Molotov handed Harriman the first formal Russian request for a postwar loan. Harriman considered the Russian proposal a "curiously worded document." Three days later he reported: "I have recovered from my surprise at Molotov's strange procedure in initiating discussions regarding a post-war credit in such a detailed *aide-mémoire* . . . ." What surprised and obviously upset Harriman was the nature of Molotov's proposal:

> The Soviet Government accordingly wishes to state the following: Having in mind the repeated statements of American public figures concerning the desirability of receiving extensive large Soviet orders for the postwar and transition period, the Soviet Government considers it possible to place orders on the basis of long-term credits to the amount of 6 billion dollars. Such orders would be for manufactured goods (oil pipes, rails, railroad cars, locomotives and other products) and industrial equipment. The credit would also cover orders for locomotives, railroad cars, rails and trucks and industrial equipment placed under Lend-Lease but not delivered to the Soviet Union before the end of the war. The credits should run for 30 years, amortization to begin on the last day of the 9th year and to end on the last day of the 30th year. Amortization should take place in the

following annual payments reckoned from end of 9th year: First 4 years $2^1/2\%$ of principal; second 4 years $3^1/2\%$; third 4 years $4^1/2\%$; fourth 4 years $5^1/2\%$; last 6 years 6%. Soviet Government will be entitled to pay up principal prematurely either in full or in part. If the two Governments decide that because of unusual and unfavorable economic conditions payment of current installments at any time might not be to mutual interest, payment may be postponed for an agreed period. Annual interest to be fixed at $2^1/2$ [$2^1/4\%$].

The United States Government should grant to Soviet Union a discount of 20% off the Government contracts with firms, of [*on*] all orders placed before end of war and falling under this credit. Prices for orders placed after the end of the war should be left to agreement between the American firms in question and Soviet representatives.

Harriman urged Washington officials to "disregard the unconventional character of the document and the unreasonableness of its terms and chalk it up to ignorance of normal business procedures and the strange ideas of the Russians on how to get the best trade." He chided the Russians for starting "negotiations on the basis of 'twice as much for half the price' . . . ." Any loan, he argued, should be dependent upon Russian behavior in overall international relations—that is, the Russians must conduct their diplomatic affairs according to American wishes and standards. "I feel strongly," he added, "that the sooner the Soviet Union can develop a decent life for its people the more tolerant they will become." But such a concern was secondary, and he demanded complete American control of the funds "in order that the political advantages may be retained and that we may be satisfied that the equipment purchased is for purposes that meet our general approval."

Harriman's response was curious and, certainly from the Russians' point of view, unreasonable. Certainly, the United States had been approached before by foreign governments with detailed requests for aid. Later, the United States was to insist that the Marshall Plan recipients do the same. Indeed, Harriman had earlier asked the Russians to be precise. And it is diplomatic practice to ask for more than one expects to get. Harriman should not have been surprised that Russia was aware of the repeated statements of American public figures concerning the desirability of receiving extensive, large Soviet orders. What perhaps disturbed him most was the boldness, thoroughness, and the attitude of independence expressed in the Russian request. He seemed fearful that the United States would fail to make political gain from the loan—that diplomatic leverage would be lost.

Assistant Secretary of State William Clayton staunchly agreed with Harriman: "From a tactical point of view, it would seem harmful to us to offer such a large credit at this time and thus lose what appears to be the only concrete bargaining lever for use in connection with the many other political and economic problems which will arise between our two countries." . . .

A week before the Yalta Conference, Grew [Assistant Secretary of State Joseph Grew] informed Harriman that the loan matter "has been discussed with the President who has displayed a keen interest and believes that it should not be pressed further pending actual discussions between himself and Stalin and other Soviet officials." Yet at Yalta in February 1945, there was virtual silence on the subject. The failure of the Roosevelt administration to discuss the loan question at length doomed postwar American reconstruction assistance to the Soviet Union, for President Harry S. Truman adopted Harriman's view after Roosevelt's death.

In an important message to the state department, in April, Harriman was pessimistic about any postwar economic cooperation with Russia. Although the Russians were "keen" to obtain a six billion dollar credit, he believed that "It certainly should be borne in mind that our basic interests might better be served by increasing our trade with other parts of the world rather than giving preference to the Soviet Union as a source of supply." The United States should undertake a domestic conservation program and end its dependence upon Soviet imports by seeking supplies in Brazil, Africa, and India. He also suggested that the President ask Congress for a blanket foreign loan program which would leave the administration the flexibility to name the recipient countries, including the Soviet Union, if agreement were possible on American terms. No credits should be extended to Russia unless the United States retained "the power to restrict or reduce them as we may see fit," he wrote, because "it is not possible to bank general goodwill in Moscow. . . ." But he cautioned: "It would be inadvisible to give the Soviets the idea that we were cooling off on our desire to help, although we should at all times make it plain that our cooperation is dependent upon a reciprocal cooperative attitude of the Soviet Government on other matters." Indeed, Harriman and Clayton both argued that the postwar loan to Russia "was the greatest element in our leverage" in Soviet-American diplomatic questions which centered on Eastern Europe, China, and Turkey. The "other matters" referred to by Harriman dealt largely with Eastern European countries, especially Poland, which were entering a Russian sphere of influence.

President Truman, generally unprepared to handle the difficult and growing foreign policy problems facing the country, relied heavily upon subordinates. On the subject of the Russian loan, the state department (Grew and Clayton in particular) and Harriman were ready to advise the President. On April 22, Truman met with Molotov in Washington to discuss the Polish question. The exchange was acrimonious, and Truman addressed Molotov as if he were a rebellious Missouri ward politician. He warned Molotov that the Russian government's international behavior would affect American decisions; "legislative appropriations were required for any economic measures in the foreign field, and I had no hope of getting such measures through Congress unless there was public support for them."

Truman's scruples about congressional impediments are not convincing. The new administration and the state department had not prepared either the public or Congress for a loan to Russia. In fact, public discussion had been discouraged. The administration had neither sought to inform public opinion nor demonstrate to the Soviet Union that the United States was willing to undertake serious negotiations on the loan question. . . .

Just before Truman left for the Potsdam Conference in July 1945, the head of the Office of War Mobilization and Reconversion, Fred Vinson, advised him that "A sound and adequate program of credits for foreign reconstruction would directly and immediately benefit the United States in both its domestic economy and its foreign policy." Vinson like many Americans feared a postwar economic slump, looked to foreign markets to take up the slack, and included the Russians in his plan for both economic and diplomatic reasons. He noted that the "Soviet Union desperately needs aid," a fact which would give Truman leverage at Potsdam. He suggested that Soviet control of Eastern Europe could be loosened by financial aid, "Our ace in the hole."

One of the items the Americans intended to discuss bilaterally with the Russians at Potsdam was "Credits to the USSR." But the subject did not come up, even though Truman later contended that he had gone there planning to offer help for Russian reconstruction. Truman said that all Stalin wanted to talk about was the ending of lend-lease. The Potsdam records do not reveal that Stalin pushed the lend-lease issue. But why did the United States fail to push the Russian loan if Truman was as prepared as he said he was to do so? . . .

In November the administration received some support from the Colmer congressional committee in its policy of using the loan as a diplomatic weapon. Its eighth report on *Economic Reconstruction in Europe* acknowledged that the Russian economy was in massive disarray and that the German "scorched earth" policy had left much of Russia in ruins. Economic cooperation with Russia should be effected, but certain points, the committee argued, should be clarified before a "sound relationship" could develop. First, the United States must be assured that any aid would not go into armaments buildup. Second, the Russians should make "a full and frank disclosure" of their production statistics. Third, Russia must withdraw its occupation forces from Eastern Europe; and, fourth, the Soviets must disclose the terms of their trade treaties with Eastern Europe. Fifth, relief should be administered on nonpolitical grounds, with no siphoning of relief supplies to Russia from Eastern Europe. And, last, before any loans were made to Eastern European countries, there must be protection for American property there. Other items mentioned also centered on the "open door": "free entry" of American planes flying ordinary Russian air routes; willingness to protect American copyrights; and the granting of visas in "adequate quantities."

Shortly after the Colmer committee report, Harriman assessed the status of the loan question. He wrote significantly and inquisitively that American economic policy toward the U. S. S. R. had "so far added to our misunderstanding and increased the Soviets [sic] recent tendency to take unilateral action." Moreover, the American loan policy "has no doubt caused them to tighten their belts as regards improvement of the living conditions of their people and *may have contributed to their avaricious policies in the countries occupied or liberated by the Red Army.*" He added that Russia worked on long-range plans and by November had probably formulated its program leaving aside American credits. Hence, any help the United States extends, he wrote, would be over and above the Soviet program. He called for a review of Soviet-American economic relations, apparently with the idea of denying Russia any further United Nations Relief and Rehabilitation Administration aid, which he thought did the United States little good, and from lend-lease, and an Export-Import Bank loan. His assessment indicated that the use of economic power as a diplomatic weapon had failed. Russia had not been swayed by such power. But, more importantly, Harriman's memorandum suggested that, had the United States earlier granted a loan to Russia, tension between the two nations might have been reduced. If he was right in his overall assessment, the United States, in its desire to use its economic power as a diplomatic weapon to gain American solutions to world issues, rather than as a negotiating tool, contributed to the schism in international relations. One correspondent from Moscow noted in early December 1945 that observers there thought that American leaders "are most interested in using that country's favorable economic position to promote United States political aims" and that Moscow publications repeatedly criticized American "dollar diplomacy" and "atom diplomacy."

A conference of the United States Economic Counselors and Advisors met in Paris from January 28 to February 2, 1946, on the subject of American economic policy toward the Soviet Union. The conference concluded that the United States should insist on full reciprocity and should be ready to withhold benefits from the Soviet Union in order to obtain reciprocity. Reciprocity at this point meant several things. Russia was supposed to open the allegedly closed trade and investment door in Eastern Europe, and it was supposed to accept American principles of international trade multilateralism as expressed in the Bretton Woods institutions, the International Bank, and the International Monetary Fund. Apparently no mention was made of Russia's political activities in Eastern Europe. Harriman's chief assistant, George F. Kennan, concluded that no loan should be made "unless they show a reciprocally cooperative attitude and give some assurance that their international trading will proceed along lines consistent with our overall approach to international economic collaboration."

On February 21, the Russian chargé in Washington was handed a note drafted by Harriman which explained that the one billion dollar credit was "one among a number of outstanding economic questions" between the United States and the Soviet Union. The note suggested negotiations and invited the Soviet Union to send observers to the first meeting of the International Monetary Fund and the International Bank scheduled for March 1946. In early March 1946, the Department of State made the false and bizarre announcement that the Russian loan request had been "lost" since August; it had been misplaced during the transference of the papers of the Foreign Economic Administration (overseer of the Export-Import Bank during and shortly after the war) to the state department. As Arthur Schlesinger, Jr., recently wrote, this "only strengthened Soviet suspicions of American purposes." What is the scholar to make of this strange announcement? The evidence is clear that the loan question was not "lost." Did the United States, because it needed a public excuse for not having pursued the loan with the Soviet Union from August to February, feign administrative clumsiness and incompetence? This question raises an even more crucial one: Why did not the Truman administration take up the matter with the Soviet Union in that period? Did the United States believe that the bargaining power of the loan was slipping and seek time to retrieve it? With the first meeting of the Bretton Woods institutions forthcoming, and with the necessity of deciding where the limited funds of the Export-Import Bank would be distributed, the administration may have considered late February the most propitious time for reviving the loan question.

The American conditions for a loan—multilateral trade policy, membership in the International Bank and the International Monetary Fund, and the open door in Eastern Europe—conflicted with Soviet policies. The Russians were not eager to assume American trade principles and to reject the state-trading practices that its economic and social system required that had been in use since the early years of the Soviet government. They were also wary of joining the International Bank and Fund, both dominated by American dollars, voting power, and leadership. Russia would have derived little economic benefit from membership and would have had to reverse a long-time reluctance to divulge details about its economy to the institutions. Nor were the Soviets willing to accept the American position that the open door—especially Russian trade treaties with the Eastern European countries—be discussed in the loan negotiations. Predictably, Russia replied to the February 21 note with a refusal to discuss her economic links with Eastern Europe; but apparently, it left the question of Bretton Woods membership in abeyance. . . .

The loan issue was not dead, however, for in May the Soviet Union, in a note to Washington, again demonstrated its interest. The American response firmly insisted that Eastern Europe be included on the agenda for negotiations and specifically protested Russian five-year trade treaties with Hungary and Rumania. With only 300 to 400 million dollars remaining in the Export-Import Bank in July, and with Congress leaving Washington to prepare for elections, there was little likelihood that the United States would grant Russia's requested loan. Clayton confirmed that the loan was virtually shelved when, a few days later, he told a Senate committee that discussions had never gone beyond "a preliminary stage." Indeed, "We've had an application but we have never agreed even on an agenda for negotiations." By October, Harriman could tell the National Press Club that the loan was no longer a "current issue." Wallace, in November, continued to call for a nonpolitical loan to Russia; and Stalin indicated in the fall of 1946 that he still hoped for economic aid from the United States. But the general question of American assistance to Russian reconstruction was seldom heard again until June of 1947, when Secretary of State George C. Marshall offered American dollars to a European recovery program. By that time the Cold War was tense, and it was clear that the Marshall Plan was to be closely supervised by Americans. Russia at first considered membership, but later summarily rejected the offer and began to tighten its grip on Eastern Europe through new trade treaties, the Molotov Plan, fixed elections, and political *coups*. . . .

The history of the abortive Russian loan posits some provocative questions. Would the Soviet Union have sought such heavy reparations from former Axis countries in Eastern Europe had a loan been granted? Harriman suggested that the Russians would not have been so "avaricious." Would there have been so much tension arising from Eastern European issues? Harriman stated that the Russians might not have followed a "unilateral" course had a loan been granted. Morgenthau argued, according to biographer John Blum, that a postwar credit to Russia would "soften the Soviet Mood on all outstanding political questions." And in June 1945, Grenville Clarke asked President Truman: "Now that Russia has regained self-confidence and military strength, it is surprising that without firm promises of aid from the United States . . . she should seek other methods of self-protection? I do not think so. On the contrary, it is inevitable and natural. This might have been mitigated if months ago we had made a treaty with Russia. . . ."

Would the Soviets have been so demanding *vis-à-vis* Germany had a loan been offered? Would they have eased up on reparation demands and have agreed early to unite the German zones if the United States had acted with speed to aid Russia, as it was later to do for Britain? One scholar writes that a loan might have taken "the acrimony out of the Russian attitude on reparations." Albert Carr concludes that "It seems altogether probable that these two matters, an American credit and German reparations, were closely linked in Soviet political thinking, for our attitude toward both questions profoundly affected the rate of Russia's postwar recovery." Indeed, as early as 1944, the American ambassador to Great Britain, John G. Winant, linked the two issues and urged Washington to assist Russian recovery. According to one of his former staff members, Winant argued "that the Russian need for material aid in repairing the vast destruction in the Soviet Union was bound to make the Soviet government particularly eager to receive reparations deliveries from Germany on a large scale." American leaders did not doubt that there was a direct connection between Russia's reparation demands and her postwar reconstruction crisis. Edwin Pauley, American reparations ambassador, wrote in 1947 that "It can be assumed . . . that Russia's intransigent position on unification and reparations is due to a desire to obtain the maximum amount of industrial and consumer goods from Germany, to meet internal political prestige needs and to help rebuild the Soviet industrial machine." Reporter Edgar Snow noted in the same year that "Ivan" was asking: "Did America offer Russia a serious alternative to reparations?" Finally, what effect would a loan have had upon the internal severities of the Russian nation? Recent indications suggest, as did Harriman earlier, that the more prosperous Russia becomes, the more attention Russian officials give to popular preferences.

At the close of World War II, Stalin told Harriman: "I will not tolerate a new *cordon sanitaire.*" The American use of the loan as a diplomatic weapon, at the same time that Great Britain was granted a handsome loan at below two percent interest, fed exaggerated Soviet fears, but fears nevertheless, that the United States was creating an international bloc and repeating post-World War I experience. As Wallace put it in a July 1946 letter to Truman:

> From the Russian point of view, also, the granting of a loan to Britain and the lack of tangible results on their request to borrow for rehabilitation purposes may be regarded as another evidence of strengthening of an anti-Soviet bloc.

The proposed American loan to Russia was never given the opportunity to demonstrate if it could serve as a peace potion for easing increasingly bitter Soviet-American relations in the 1945-1946 period. From the Soviet point of view, the American insistent requests for both a politically and economically "open door" in Eastern Europe, for Soviet acceptance of American multilateral most-favored-nation trade principles, and for Soviet membership in the Bretton Woods institutions, seemed to require capitulation of national interest and security concerns. From the American point of view, Soviet failure to concede these issues endangered the American conception of postwar peace and prosperity. In order to fulfill that conception, the Truman administration—over the objections of Morgenthau, Nelson, White, and Wallace, among others—decided to employ the loan as a diplomatic *weapon before* negotiations began rather than as a diplomatic *tool at* the conference table. Few nations or individuals are eager to enter negotiations when the attitude of the other party is simplistically "Our way or not at all." The diplomatic use of economic power by any nation possessing it is to be expected and can conceivably be helpful in achieving fruitful and mutually beneficial negotiations. But if that power thwarts negotiations or is employed to buttress demands which alone are held to be the *sine qua non* for peaceful settlement, the result is schism and conflict.

GABRIEL KOLKO
The Politics of War

IN DEFINING "United States Interests and Policy" in Eastern Europe, Stettinius, Hull's successor, at the beginning of November outlined the basic American position for an always receptive Roosevelt:

1. The right of peoples to choose and maintain for themselves without outside interference the type of political, social, and economic systems they desire. . . .
2. Equality of opportunity, as against the setting up of a policy of exclusion, in commerce, transit, and trade; and freedom to negotiate, either through government agencies or private enterprise, irrespective of the type of economic system in operation.
3. The right of access to all countries on an equal and unrestricted basis of . . . press, radio, newsreel and information agencies. . . .
4. Freedom for American philanthropic and educational organizations. . . .
5. General protection of American citizens and the protection and furtherance of legitimate American economic rights, existing or potential.
6. The United States maintains the general position that territorial settlements should be left until the end of the war.[1]

The dimensions of this policy, which became the basic formulation of United States objectives in Eastern Europe, ignored the conflict between the implications of the first point and the others that followed, much less the fact that United States interference in the internal affairs of France, Italy, and elsewhere was well established by this time. Indeed, as Stettinius suggested in his fifth principle, Americans could make future investments only within the context of a capitalist economy at least some of the Eastern European nations might not wish to continue; and the settlement of territorial questions, in addition to resisting British and Russian

[1]*Foreign Relations of the United States, United States Department of State (Washington, D.C., 1861–) 1944, IV, pp. 1025–26.*

Mr. Kolko is Professor of History at York University in Canada.

policy, ignored the equity of self-determination implied in the first point. The inconsistencies of this formulation were less significant than the tangible demands for an open door to the Eastern European economies. . . .

The type of politics the United States wished to see emerge in Eastern Europe assumed that the Eastern European masses would and should welcome back the prewar parties, and indeed that the holocaust of war had not gravely undermined and debilitated these parties. Moreover, the essential foreign policy of the prewar centrist parties had been anti-Soviet, irredentist, and expansionist. The Russians would not tolerate them, nor would the masses, who were not always Communist but very much for long-overdue radical social changes in one form or another. In fact the Americans appreciated this mood, but at no time did they bother to formulate a policy on the land problem so critical not only to the petite bourgeoisie but also to the larger majority that would unquestionably prevail either by a democratic vote or leftist totalitarianism. Throughout most of Eastern Europe the urban middle class was now a mere aspiration, for their irrational leaders had encouraged two wars which had resulted in the destruction of middle-class property. To suggest that social revolution in Eastern Europe was exclusively a product of Soviet intervention, much less that it was not needed, ignored the structural facts and accepted the argument of the advocates of a prewar status quo that was bankrupt and had perpetuated wide-scale misery far greater than that incident to sweeping social changes and broad internal economic and political development. The existence of Soviet power in Eastern Europe permitted more or less natural and indigenous forces to take their logical course, while in Western Europe, American and British power contained these forces directly or indirectly, a containment that became the preeminent unifying element in the Western alliance after 1945, and which also hindered postwar economic recovery. The mere fact that there was no serious internal opposition to the Communization of Eastern Europe, that is, no significant civil wars, reflected both the fundamental weakness of the Old Order (and suggests what kind of system they would have re-created without a mass base) and the flexibility and subtlety of the various Communist parties and the Russians.

Although it ruled together with England in the West with an iron hand, the United States called for free elections and self-rule in Eastern Europe at this time, but prewar precedents convinced the Russians that the West sought to create an anti-Soviet bloc. Unfettered democracy never existed in Eastern Europe outside Czechoslovakia; the prewar parties were venal, weak, or both; and the region needed a period of development on new social bases, with its dangerous nationalism contained, to prevent Europe from plunging into more irrational wars on behalf of the cause of Serbs, Macedonians, and the like. The American planners ignored these nationality questions, since they had no specific or new proposals to make. The Soviet role in shaping Eastern European politics may have been in the name of a cynical ideology, but Eastern Europe, it was clear by the end of 1944, was going to go right *or* left, into an anti-Soviet bloc, a pro-Soviet bloc, or true neutrality. The Russians would tolerate only the last two options, the United States only the first, and the British, with much twisting and turning, opted for neutralism more often than not. American diplomacy, in calling for the restoration of prewar politics and economics, worked for the Right, which quickly came to view the Americans as its last hope. Russia would not, and was not obliged to, tolerate this development.

The Americans had to work for the restoration of the London Poles, Mihailovic, and other conservatives because their economic objectives, which by the end of 1944 they clearly defined as primary, were incompatible with radical economic reform in Eastern Europe. Eighty percent of Eastern Europe's exports in 1938 consisted of raw materials, foodstuffs, and semifinished goods, and nearly three-quarters of it went to Western Europe.[2] To talk of the restoration of stability, normal trade, and the reintegration of Eastern Europe into the world economy meant, in effect, the continuation of the semicolonial economic relationship of that area to the rest of the world. Any alteration of this condition would have meant radical internal economic changes, and this in turn would have impinged on American freedom to invest and trade along traditional lines so central to its objectives in that area. If the United States chose to approach Eastern European problems from this viewpoint, it would find no satisfaction, for every important left-of-center group, Beneš' exile government included, favored far-

---

[2]U.S. Senate, Committee on Foreign Relations, *A Background Study on East-West Trade.* 89:1. April, 1965 (Washington, 1965) 1–2.

reaching nationalization and economic reform. To make this the test of Eastern European friendship condemned the area to hostility unless it would restore the prewar politicians. And, as history proved, between the pressures of Western hostility and the final consolidation of Russian power in Eastern Europe after 1947; this policy spelled the end of Czech democracy. Nationalization and independent economic development along new lines became the critical gauge by which the Americans evaluated Eastern European trends, for politics was only the instrument for preserving and expanding America's unprecedented power and position in the European and world economy. When the State Department reconsidered and clarified its Eastern European policy before Yalta, in essence it defined a foreign economic policy. . . .

The problem of Soviet power gradually subsumed the other great wartime challenge to American diplomacy: the emergence of the Left and its threat to securing American economic and political war aims. In Eastern Europe, perhaps more than any other single region, American leaders found evidence of what they interpreted to be the dangers of Soviet expansionism that might undercut the attainment of their nation's largest postwar goals. The war utterly and finally destroyed the traditional Eastern European political and economic structure and nothing the Russians might do could alter that fact, for not the Soviet Union but the leaders of the Old Order in Eastern Europe themselves made that collapse inevitable. The Russians could work within that new structural limitation in a variety of ways, and in practice they did explore many political options, but they could not transcend the new socioeconomic reality. More aware than anyone else of their own weaknesses in the event of a conflict with the United States, the Russians pursued a conservative and cautious line wherever they could find local non-Communist groups willing to abjure the traditional diplomacy of the cordon sanitaire and anti-Bolshevism. They were entirely willing to restrain equally the militant Left and militant Right, and given the complex political admixtures of the region they showed neither more nor less respect for an unborn functional democracy in Eastern Europe than the Americans and British evidenced in Italy, Greece, or Belgium. For neither the Americans, British, nor Russians were willing to permit democracy to run its course anywhere in Europe at the cost of damaging their vital strategic and economic interests, perhaps also bringing about the triumph of the Left or the restoration of prewar clerical fascism. In fact we now know that the Russians lost control of the revolutionary forces in Yugoslavia and Greece, and that they had no intention of Bolshevizing Eastern Europe in 1945 if—but only if—they could find alternatives.

For the United States, Eastern Europe was a question of economic war aims to which political realities had also to conform to satisfy American aspirations, and quite apart from the local leaderships' policies toward Russia, that was hardly possible in nearly all the Eastern European nations. Even where the United States had yet to develop all of its objectives in specific detail, it was imperative that it prevent any Great Power from totally dominating Eastern Europe or any other region of the world for that matter, because the United States considered all political and economic blocs or spheres of influence that it did not control as directly undermining its larger political, and especially economic, objectives for an integrated world capitalism and a political structure which was the prerequisite to its goals. For this reason America opposed Britain's control over French affairs and set itself against an Eastern European reality which neither it, nor in the last analysis, the Russians, could fully shape according to a plan or desire.

Given the pervasive, chronic Russian conservatism on political questions during the war, one best reflected in the United Front tactics of accommodation which caused the Russian-disciplined Left to submerge its distinctive socialist character at all costs, the failure to reach agreement over Poland or Czechoslovakia—and Eastern Europe in general—reflected the effort of the United States to disengage Soviet influence in Eastern Europe and to create states ready to cooperate with a postwar economic program compatible with American objectives and interests. To the Russians during the war, Eastern Europe was a question of preventing the resurrection of traditionally hostile conservative leaders, and in this they had the total collapse of much of Eastern European society working on their behalf. To the Americans it was a matter of putting together a perhaps somewhat reformed version of the social and political sources of Eastern Europe's alliance with atavistic forces of imperialism and nationalism during two wars and reintegrating the region into a traditional prewar European economy in a condition of semicolonialism. That task was beyond the power of the United States or Russia, but it was a failure of American policy for which Washington was ultimately to hold Russia responsible. This exacerbation of world politics over Eastern Europe was a result of American expansion into the historically hopeless imbroglio and mire of Eastern European affairs.

In the last analysis both the Soviet Union and the United States could only partially control the uncontrollable—the Left—and could seemingly inhibit it only in Western Europe. For World War II brought to fruition a whole spectrum of internal crises inherent in the civil war in society, which was a by-product of different admixtures within each nation of industrial capitalism, World War I, and the continued weakening of world capitalism and colonialism after 1939. America, with some significant aid from Russia, might retard that collapse, yet it could not stay its irresistible momentum, and all the issues were joined during the period 1942–1945 that were again to break out with renewed force after the war to define the direction of modern world diplomacy and conflict. The Old Order of prewar capitalism and oligarchy with which the United States identified, with reservations, and which it hoped to reform and integrate into a transformed world capitalist economy, was dying in the colonial world and a dependent China; it committed suicide in Eastern Europe, and the United States could refurbish it in temporarily acceptable ways only in Western Europe. The impact of these changes on the conditions and structure of world power ultimately were to be more far-reaching than the Bolshevik Revolution itself, in part because—after 1947—the protective existence and support of Soviet power was a cushion between success and failure in many, but by no means all, socialist or revolutionary nations. . . .

It is this deliberate quality, this articulate set of economic and political goals which ultimately set the Untted States at the end of World War II against the Soviet Union, against the tide of the Left, and against Britain as a coequal guardian of world capitalism—in fact, against history as it had been and had yet to become. That there was something accidental or unintended about the American response to the world is a comforting reassurance to those who wish to confuse the American rhetoric and descriptions of intentions with the realities and purposes of operational power, but given the society and its needs American foreign policy could hardly have been different. For the United States emerged from the war with a sense of vast power, and indeed, as the most powerful single state in the world, anxious to attain a highly organized world economic and political community as a precondition to the realization of its vital peace aims. But as strong as it was, the United States, even when the Soviet Union worked with it for its own reasons and toward its own ends, was too weak to mold the destiny of mankind everywhere on earth. It might limit and shape that fate, but it could not control the world by creating its desired political and economic order modeled after American aspirations.

At times the key decision-makers in Washington fully appreciated America's possible inadequacy and need for allies, as in their enigmatic attitudes toward the future of Germany in Europe and Japan in the Far East. Everywhere in the world America could deploy material power in various forms, and at the conference table it spoke with a weight beyond that of any other state. Estimating this strength in relation to that of other states, Washington fully intended that at the end of the war America could, and would, determine the basic character of the postwar world. For this reason Roosevelt and his aides throughout 1943 and 1944 opposed the desire of the British Foreign Office to meet Soviet aims in Eastern Europe at the bargaining table, for the leaders of the United States fully expected—and this was as true of Roosevelt as of Truman—to employ American power to define the political and economic outcome of the war when their allies were relatively weak. The problem, which it was impossible for anyone in Washington to sufficiently perceive and appreciate, was that the kind of world emerging from the war required power beyond the factory and army, the kind of resources and inspiration that only revolutionary movements in villages and mountains can possess and generate.

For insofar as world conflict was transformed from wars between states into ideological and civil wars for social transformation and liberation, the political arithmetic of sheer insufficiency of numbers made it impossible for the Americans to be everywhere at once, and to employ vast technological power—in bases and ships the Americans planned to have throughout the world—against sheer mass. To succeed in that situation one had to be neither American, English, nor Russian, but to be present in every village in the hungry world, or, as in the case of the Russians, to endorse an inevitability that they could neither initiate nor prevent.

It was in this context of vast material might and yet greater ambition that World War II ended for the United States and defined the manner in which the postwar period began. There was nothing qualitatively unique about this goal or the tools that the United States employed, for the reliance on the state to attain the domestic and international objectives of private American business interests, or to advance a broader "national interest" on behalf of an allegedly new internationalism which scarcely concealed the imperial intent behind it, much less the consequences, was a characteristic of American life and had been for many decades. What was new was the vastly more destructive technology which now accompanied the expansion of states—of which the United States was both the most powerful and first after 1943—and the human consequences of international conflicts.

WILLIAM APPLEMAN WILLIAMS
The Tragedy of American Diplomacy

ROOSEVELT'S IDEA OF reaching an accommodation with Stalin was not based on some utopian dream of perfect and everlasting agreement on any and all issues. However, Roosevelt simply did not understand the nature and workings of a modern, complex industrial economy. The result in domestic affairs was that his political acumen and skill were never focused on the central and vital issues of getting the political economy into some kind of fundamentally dynamic balance. The same weakness plagued him in dealing with the Russians. He never got his priorities straight. Short of war, economic aid was the one effective tool he had in negotiations with the Soviets. But he never used it.

Roosevelt's successors understood and used that lever, but they treated it as a weapon to force the Soviets to accept American policies. The conflict over affairs in eastern Europe which developed out of that attitude is usually stressed in discussing the origins of the cold war. Yet it may be that the issues of German reparations and American expansion in the Middle East were equally important as determining factors. Failing to obtain a loan from America, Stalin had to decide between three possible courses of action.

He could give way and accept the American interpretation of all disputed points, abandoning foreign communists to their fate and attempting to control the extremists in his own nation. He could respond with an orthodox revolutionary program throughout the world. Or, relying on large economic reparations from Germany, he could continue the effort to resolve his dilemma in a conservative manner even though he did not have any formal understanding with the United States. This approach would also do much to keep Germany from becoming a threat to Russia in the immediate future. It left him, however, with the need to effect some basic settlement concerning eastern Europe, the Far East, and the Black Sea

Mr. Williams is Professor of History at Oregon State University.

region. . . .

Despite his failure to get any positive response from the United States on the question of a postwar loan, or a clear understanding on other vital issues, Stalin still hoped to effect a conservative resolution of his dilemma. Throughout the first half of 1945, for example, *Izvestia* stressed the vitality of the American economy (in striking contrast to the fears being expressed in Congressional hearings), emphasized the importance of resolving outstanding issues by negotiation, and reiterated the fruitfulness of economic cooperation. The British press attaché in Russia reported that Soviet comment remained restrained and hopeful until America initiated a campaign of vigorous criticism and protest aimed at Soviet predominance in eastern Europe. . . .

Soviet officials who later chose to live in the West often offered the same kind of evidence bearing on Russian policy at the end of the war. One of the American experts who interviewed many such men offered this general judgment about Soviet policy in Germany. "The paramount consideration was not the extension of the revolution to Germany and the establishment of a Soviet Government there, but the rehabilitation of the Soviet Union's war-ravaged industry and transportation . . . regardless of the effect this policy might have on . . . establishing a Soviet Germany." For that matter, the Red Army's railroad lines across Poland into Germany were ripped up in 1945. And in eastern Europe, the Soviet approach was modeled on the popular front governments of the 1930's rather than upon the existing Soviet system.

The point of these examples (and there are many more) is not to suggest, let alone try to prove, that Stalin and other Soviet leaders behaved either as Western democrats or as men uninterested in exercising influence in eastern Europe. The point is to indicate and to stress the importance of three quite different things: first, the very significant extent to which Soviet decisions from 1944 through 1947 were based on domestic Russian conditions; second, the degree to which the Soviets were assuming that capitalism would stabilize itself around the great and undamaged power of the United States; and third, the way in which those two factors pointed in the mind of many Russians—including Stalin—to the need to reach some kind of agreement with America. They never defined such an understanding on the basis of abandoning Russian influence in eastern Europe or acquiescing in each and every American proposal just as it first emanated from Washington. But neither did they emerge from World War II with a determination to take over eastern Europe and then embark upon a cold war with the United States.

Beginning in 1946, Stalin grew ever more skeptical about the possibility of negotiating any basic understanding with American leaders. But he never became a fatalist about war with the United States. And the so-called softies in the party were not finally downgraded, and then subjected to vigorous and extensive attacks (including imprisonment) until the late summer and early fall of 1947. It was not until even later that the Soviet Union moved ruthlessly to extend and consolidate its control over eastern Europe.

Stalin's effort to solve Russia's problem of security and recovery short of widespread conflict with the United States was not matched by American leaders who acceded to power upon the death of Roosevelt. The President bequeathed them little, if anything, beyond the traditional outlook of open-door expansion. They proceeded rapidly and with a minimum of debate to translate that conception of America and the world into a series of actions and policies which closed the door to any result but the cold war.

The various themes which went into America's conception of the freedom and the necessity of open-door expansion, from the doctrine of the elect to the frontier thesis, had been synthesized into an ideology before Roosevelt's death. Once it was frozen into ideology, it became very difficult—and perhaps artificial, even then—to assign priorities to its various facets. Even a single man, let alone a group, emphasized different themes at various times. Yet the open-door outlook was based on an economic definition of the world, and this explanation of reality was persistently stressed by America's corporate leadership as it developed its policy toward the Soviet Union and other nations. It was not the possession of the atomic bomb which prompted American leaders to get tough with Russia but rather their open-door outlook which interpreted the bomb as the final guarantee that they could go further faster down that path to world predominance.

Long before anyone knew that the bomb would work, most American leaders were operating on the basis of three assumptions or ideas which defined the world in terms of a cold war. The first specified Russia as being evil but weak. . . .

Even before the end of the war in Europe, many Americans were again comparing Stalin with Hitler and stressing the importance of avoiding any repetition of the appeasement of Nazi Germany. Others, like John Foster Dulles, who had sought persistently and until a very late date to reach a broad compromise with Hitler and Japan, changed their approach when it came to dealing with Russia. They made no such efforts to reach an understanding with Stalin. And by the time of the San Francisco Conference on the United Nations, such leaders as Averell Harriman were publicly expressing their view that there was an "irreconcilable difference" between Russia and the Western powers.

At the same time, however, very few—if any—American leaders thought that Russia would launch a war. Policy-makers were quite aware of the "pitiful" conditions in western Russia, of the nation's staggering losses and its general exhaustion, of its "simply enormous" need for outside help "to repair the devastation of war," and of Stalin's stress on firm economic and political agreements with the United States to provide the basis for that reconstruction. In their own discussions, American decision-makers drew an astute and crucial distinction between Soviet actions to establish a security perimeter in eastern Europe and an all-out aggressive move against the entire capitalist world. They were right in their estimate that Russia was concerned with the first objective. They were also correct in concluding that the Soviet Union—unlike Nazi Germany—"is not essentially constructed as a dynamic expansionist state."

Far from emphasizing the imminence of a Russian attack, American leaders stressed the importance of denying any and all Soviet requests or overtures of a revised strategic agreement in the Middle East, and at the same time concentrated on reasserting American influence in eastern Europe while pushing the Russians back to their traditional borders. The first such American action came in the spring and summer of 1945 in the form of protests over Soviet influence that developed as the Red Army moved westward in pursuit of the Nazis. These protests were not prompted by the fear that Russia was about to overwhelm Europe or the world in general, but rather by the traditional outlook of the open door and the specific desire to keep the Soviets from establishing any long-range influence in eastern Europe.

Another basic attitude held by American leaders defined the United States as the symbol and the agent of positive good as opposed to Soviet evil and assumed that the combination of American strength and Russian weakness made it possible to determine the future of the world in accordance with that judgment. One important congressional leader, for example, remarked in 1943 that lend-lease provided the United States with a "wonderful opportunity" to bring the United States to "a greater degree of determining authority" in the world. He was quite aware that his view was "shared by some of the members of the President's Cabinet" and that important State Department officials were "fully in accord" with the same outlook. Another key congressman was thinking in terms of the "United States seeking world power as a trustee for civilization." Following the even earlier lead of publisher Henry R. Luce, who had announced in 1941 that it was high noon of the American Century, various business spokesmen began stressing the need to become "missionaries of capitalism and democracy. . . . "

The third essential aspect of the open-door outlook, which also made its appearance before the end of the war, was the fear that America's economic system would suffer a serious depression if it did not continue to expand overseas. Stressing the fact that there remained roughly nine million unemployed in 1940, one leading New Deal senator warned in 1943 that the danger of another depression could not be overemphasized. A government economic expert promptly supported this view with his own report that "it unfortunately is a fact that for the majority of the people in the United States the thing we have liked to refer to as the American standard of living is only possible in situations where two people in the family are working." . . .

As it moved quickly to take over the government affairs after the death of Roosevelt, the Truman Administration made it clear that it would sustain all these aspects of the traditional approach to foreign policy. "The United States cannot reach and maintain the high level of employment we have set as our goal," Secretary of State James

F. Byrnes reiterated, "unless the outlets for our production are larger than they've ever been before in peacetime." . . .

President Harry S. Truman was for his part an enthusiastic and militant advocate of America's supremacy in the world. He seemed, indeed, to react, think, and act as an almost classic personification of the entire Open Door Policy. From a very early date, moreover, he led the rapid revival of the analogy between Nazi Germany and the Soviet Union (and Hitler and Stalin) which became one of the fundamental clichés of America's analysis of the postwar world. Given that analogy, which was very rapidly and very generally accepted, American policy can without much exaggeration be described as an effort to establish the Open Door Policy once and for all by avoiding what were judged—on the basis of the analogy— to have been the errors of appeasement made during the 1930's.

There were two central fallacies involved in that estimate of the world. Soviet Russia and Nazi Germany were significantly different in crucial aspects of domestic and foreign policy; and, unlike the situation in the 1930's, the United States was neither weak nor disarmed. Indeed, it enjoyed a great absolute as well as relative advantage in both economic and military power. As the United States Government candidly admitted even as late as 1962, the United States had been the strongest power in the world ever since 1944. For that matter, it was the existence and the knowledge of that strength that encouraged Truman and other leaders after 1945 to think that they could force the Soviets to accept American proposals without recourse to war.

It is no doubt wrong and inaccurate to conclude that the effort to establish the false analogy between Soviet Russia and Nazi Germany was the product of conscious distortion by America's private and official leaders. Many of them adopted and used that argument in complete sincerity. They simply accepted it without serious thought or critical evaluation. However mistaken in fact and logic, such men were not hypocrites. But it also is true that there were a good many men who shared the attitude of Senator Arthur K. Vandenberg. He thought it was necessary "to scare hell out of the American people" in order to win their active approval and support for the kind of vigorous anti-Soviet policy he wanted. Those men did consciously employ exaggeration and oversimplification to accomplish their objectives. Senator Taft would seem to have offered a sound judgment on that conduct. He remarked during congressional consideration of the European Recovery Program that he was more than a bit tired of having the Russian menace invoked as a reason for doing any-and everything that might or might not be desirable or necessary on its own merits.

Truman not only thought about Russia in terms of Nazi Germany, but he made it clear very soon after he took the oath as President that he intended to reform the world on American terms. He casually told one early visitor "that the Russians would soon be put in their places; and that the United States would then take the lead in running the world in the way that the world ought to be run." Then, on April 23, 1945, he told the Cabinet "that he felt our agreements with the Soviet Union so far had been a one-way street and that he could not continue; it was now or never. He intended to go on with the plans for [the] San Francisco [Conference] and if the Russians did not wish to join us they could go to hell." Senator Vandenberg, soon to become (along with John Foster Dulles) the Republican leader of that bipartisan approach to the Soviet Union, caught the spirit—and reflected the absurd exaggeration—of the outlook of his diary entry of the following day: "FDR's appeasement of Russia is over."

As one insider remarked, "the strong view prevailed" from the very beginning, though it did not take on the form and tone of a great crusade against the Soviet Union and international communism until the end of 1946. Thus, for example, additional lend-lease allocations and shipments to Russia were canceled in May 1945. The full story of the cancellation has never been revealed. In the narrow sense, the action can be interpreted as a blunder. Truman later referred to it as "my greatest mistake," and claimed that, given a second chance, he would have handled it differently. Nevertheless, all lend-lease to the Soviets was closed off promptly once the Japanese surrendered. It is also clear that, on a comparative basis, Russia was treated far less considerately than England and France during the process of termination. In those respects, therefore, the action was repeated.

But in the first instance, and as Truman later explained, the authority to act had been sought by Leo Crowley, the Foreign

Economic Administrator, who proceeded to interpret it very broadly and to use it very vigorously. Truman's oblique comment that the whole affair was "clearly a case of policy-making on the part of Crowley and Grew" implies an explanation that can be substantiated by other evidence. Crowley's push for the power was supported by Admiral William D. Leahy, Assistant Secretary of State Joseph Grew, and Harriman. All those men wanted to use American economic power to coerce the Soviets on policy issues. This is established beyond any question in a Grew memorandum of his phone conversation with Crowley on May 12, 1945, as they were working to obtain a grant of authority from Truman. The document makes it absolutely clear that Crowley and Grew had Russia in the very forefront of their minds as they pressured the President. For his own part, Crowley refused to consider the Russian request for a loan as coming under the lend-lease law, even though he did negotiate such an arrangement involving $9 million with France. Crowley's general outlook was revealed when congressmen questioned him about loans in general. "If you did not like the government," he was asked, "you would not have to make them a loan at all?" "That is right," Crowley replied. "If you create good governments in foreign countries, automatically you will have better markets for ourselves."

Whatever further details may ultimately be added to the story of the termination, there is no doubt that the action seriously antagonized the Russians. Stalin interpreted it as a move to put pressure on him to accept American policies, and bluntly called it "disturbing." Then, in a very revealing series of comments, Stalin told Harry Hopkins in May 1945 that such an approach would not produce Soviet acquiescence.

Stalin first provided an insight into the differences within the Soviet hierarchy. The Russian leader said that "he would not attempt to use Soviet public opinion as a screen but would speak of the feeling that had been created in Soviet governmental circles as a result of recent moves on the part of the United States Government." "These circles felt a certain alarm," he explained, "in regard to the attitude of the United States Government. It was their impression that the American attitude towards the Soviet Union had perceptibly cooled once it became obvious that Germany was defeated, and that it was as though the Americans were saying that the Russians were no longer needed."

To be specific, Stalin continued, the way lend-lease had been cancelled "had been unfortunate and even brutal . . . [and] had caused concern to the Soviet Government. If the refusal to continue lend-lease was designed as pressure on the Russians in order to soften them up, then it was a fundamental mistake."

In this episode involving lend-lease, as well as in additional examples reported by Truman, Byrnes, and other American leaders, Molotov emerges as the leader and spokesman of the militant wing of the Soviet hierarchy. It should be remembered in this connection that Molotov caught the full impact of Truman's vehement anti-Soviet attitude in a face-to-face meeting on April 23, 1945, that followed the crucial discussion of that policy among American leaders on the same day. There is considerable and convincing evidence, furthermore, that Molotov often took and persisted in a very tough line with the United States until Stalin intervened to modify and soften the Russian position. This interpretation of the disagreements among Soviet leaders is further and dramatically reinforced by events after Stalin's death, and particularly by the continued agitation by Molotov against Premier Nikita S. Khrushchev's efforts to establish the policy of co-existence and peaceful transition to socialism and communism.

In 1945, as in later situations of a similar nature, the position of Molotov and his supporters was unquestionably strengthened by the actions of the United States. Stalin was broadly justified in his fears expressed to Hopkins about the developing American attitude concerning the importance of Russia after the defeat of Germany. Truman and his advisors did not immediately and drastically downgrade Russian help. They continued to seek Soviet assistance against the Japanese until they learned that the atom bomb was a success. At that point, their attitude changed drastically: they clearly wanted to defeat Japan before the Russians entered the war. Even before that, however, at the end of April 1945, the change had begun to occur. Following the meeting of April 23, for example, the United States stopped pressing for air bases in Siberia, and ceased worrying about clearing the North Pacific shipping lanes to Russia's far eastern ports. In a similar way, American position papers prepared for the forthcoming meeting with Stalin at Potsdam revealed a determination to push for the open door in eastern Europe. . . .

Following upon President Roosevelt's clear expression of a desire to retain "complete freedom of action," the United States Government under President Truman initiated and sustained a vigorous drive to undercut the Stalin-Churchill agreement of October 1944, concerning eastern Europe, and to replace it with the Open Door Policy. Churchill supported that determined effort to subvert the understanding which he himself had originally and voluntarily written out and pushed across the table to Stalin. Truman and Churchill undertook that course, moreover, in the full knowledge and open acknowledgement that Stalin had honored his part of the bargain in Greece.

This insistence upon applying the Open Door Policy to eastern Europe (and, of course, to Asia) was decided upon before anyone knew for sure that the atom bomb would work. Along with the feeling among American policy-makers that Russia's war-caused weakness would enable them to secure major concessions from Moscow, that consideration must be kept constantly in mind when following the sequence of events after the defeat of Germany. The success of the bomb strengthened an existing attitude and a traditional strategy—it did not call forth a new approach. . . .

Stalin arrived in Potsdam with a noticeably different set of priorities. He was still concerned about Russia's frontiers in Europe, about preventing Germany from trying it all over in another 25 years, and about a major economic transfusion for the Soviet Union's battered economy. Apparently shrewd enough to realize that he had but little chance to obtain a large loan from the United States, and in any event unable to plan on that basis in the summer of 1945, Stalin laid immediate and heavy emphasis on being treated as an equal and upon obtaining massive reparations from Germany and its former allies. . . .

Molotov connected the issues of reparations and German war potential very simply: "The question of reparations was even more urgent because unless this was settled there could be no progress on economic matters" involving the future strength of German industry. Hence the Soviets wanted "clear replies to the questions."

Byrnes gave them one by suddenly remarking that the United States now considered the Yalta figure of 10 billions for Russia to be "impractical." Molotov then shot back that the Soviets were "entitled to a clear answer" on what figure the United States did find acceptable. . . .

Finally, in the face of continued American refusal to discuss the issues in that related way, Stalin accepted the Byrnes proposal of July 23, 1945. He then extended it in a way that clearly foreshadowed the division of Europe. The specific issue involved the assignment of German assets in other European countries, but the discussion immediately picked up overtones of a far broader nature.

> PREMIER STALIN: . . . with regard to shares and foreign investments, perhaps the demarcation lines between the Soviet and Western zones of occupation should be taken as the dividing lines and everything west of that line would go to the Allies and everything east of that line to the Russians.
>
> THE PRESIDENT [TRUMAN] inquired if he meant a line running from the Baltic to the Adriatic.
>
> PREMIER STALIN replied in the affirmative. . . .
>
> [BRITISH FOREIGN SECRETARY] BEVIN said he agreed and asked if Greece would belong to Britain. . . .
>
> PREMIER STALIN suggested that the Allies take Yugoslavia and Austria would be divided into zones. . . .
>
> MR. BYRNES said he thought it was important to have a meeting of minds. Mr. Bevin's question was whether the Russians' claim was limited to the zone occupied by the Russian Army. To that he understood Mr. Stalin to say 'yes.' If that were so he was prepared to agree.
>
> PREMIER STALIN replied in the affirmative. . . .
>
> THE PRESIDENT [TRUMAN] said that he agreed with the Soviet proposal.

The American decision to give the Russians a free hand on reparations throughout eastern Europe can in the end be explained only in one of three ways. The first would be to assert that the United States knowingly handed eastern Europe over to the Soviet Union. This is absurd on the face of it. It is also belied by Truman's actions during the conference, and by his blunt public remarks after the meeting was over. The eastern European countries, he announced on August 9, 1945; were "not to be spheres of influence of any one power." The Open Door Policy was thereby reaffirmed. A second explanation would be based on the idea that the United States made the reparations deal without understanding its political implications. But that interpretation is undercut by the analyses prepared by Clayton and other American officials who did see those possibilities.

The third explanation is supported by direct and indirect evidence. It is, simply, that the United States—confident in its vast economic and military superiority over Russia—made the reparations agreement to avoid any indirect financing of Soviet recovery. American leaders were certain that the bomb, and Russia's great recovery needs, provided them with the leverage to re-establish the Open Door, and pro-Western governments, in eastern Europe. . . .

. . . Specifically, Byrnes was "disturbed" by, and sought to limit or stop completely, the Soviet moves to establish close economic partnerships with eastern European nations. In the positive sense, he sustained Truman's drive launched during the Potsdam meeting to internationalize the entire Danubian waterway system.

That move of Truman and Byrnes in 1945 was in many respects similar and comparable to Secretary of State Knox's attempt in 1909 to internationalize the Manchurian railway system. The analogy is illuminating. The American objective was the same in both cases: as the London *Times* described the postwar maneuver, to establish the conditions under which there would be "free entry into the Danube Valley and Eastern Europe for the goods and capital of the Western countries." And just as it had been assumed in Manchuria, so it was also assumed in eastern Europe in 1945 that such free access for American economic power would in turn help to create and sustain political predominance. The American demand for free elections in eastern Europe was considered by American policy-makers as much a means to such economic and political ends as a philosophic or moral end in and of itself.

But as Knox had failed in 1909, so did Byrnes fail in 1945. As they had done in 1909, the Russians in 1945 evaluated the American proposal for exactly what it was. And as in the earlier episode, so also in the later one—the Russians resisted. One exchange between Byrnes and Molotov summarized not only the impasse at London in 1945, but much of the diplomacy of the succeeding 15 years. The

Secretary of State tried to persuade Molotov that the United States, despite its demands for the Open Door and its refusal to come to terms on reparations, was not trying to weaken or close out Soviet influence in eastern Europe. "I must tell you," Molotov replied, "I have my doubts as to this."

The New York *Times* correspondent Herbert L. Matthews wrote from London on September 25, 1945, what probably remains the best short analysis of what happened between the spring and the early fall of that fateful year. "France, Britain, and the United States, in seeking to absorb eastern Europe into a unified continental system, are aiming to weaken the Eastern bloc, and at the same time they are being forced with varying degrees of reluctance into the formation of that very Western block that Russia dreads.

"It is a vicious circle. . . . "

DENNA F. FLEMING
The Cold War and Its Origins

THE TRUMAN DOCTRINE AND ITS RECEPTION

THE PRESIDENT READ the message to a joint session of the two Houses of Congress on March 12, in an even monotone. He received light applause at three points. For the most part the Congress listened grimly and silently. On the same morning the *New York Times* had predicted that Truman would "ring down the curtain on one epoch in America's foreign policy." As he read, there could be no doubt that this was the case.

In Greece, said the President, "a militant minority, exploiting human want and misery was able to create political chaos which until now, has made economic recovery impossible." The "terroristic activities of several thousand armed men, led by communists," had created a situation with which the Greek Government could not cope. We had considered how the United Nations might help, but the situation was urgent and the United Nations and its related organizations were not in a position to extend help "of the kind that is required."

Turkey also deserved our attention. It had been spared the disasters of war but needed modernization. Its integrity was essential to the preservation of order in the Middle East.

We could not "realize our objectives," unless we were "willing to help free people to maintain their free institutions and their national integrity against aggressive movements that seek to impose upon them totalitarian regimes." This had happened, in spite of our frequent protests and in violation of the Yalta Agreement, in Poland, Bulgaria, Rumania and other countries. The time had come when "nearly every nation must choose between alternative ways of life," one distinguished by free institutions and the other by terror and oppression. He believed "that *it must be the policy of the United States to support free peoples who are resisting attempted subjugation by armed minorities or by outside pressure."* [Italics added.]

Mr. Fleming is Professor of International Relations at Vanderbilt University.

Excerpts from D. F. Fleming, *The Cold War and Its Origins,* Doubleday & Company, Inc.

"If Greece should fall under the control of an armed minority," confusion and disorder might spread east throughout the entire Middle East and west through the countries of Europe. He therefore asked for four hundred million dollars for Greece and Turkey and authority to detail civilian and military personnel to them.

All Revolution Forbidden. No pronouncement could have been more sweeping. Wherever a communist rebellion developed the United States would suppress it. Wherever the Soviet Union attempted to push outward, at any point around its vast circumference, the United States would resist. The United States would become the world's anti-communist, anti-Russian policeman.

This, too, was not the full extent of the Doctrine, for its all inclusive language also forbade every kind of revolution, democratic or otherwise. It would be difficult to find a revolution anywhere which had not been the work of an armed minority. The people might later come to the support of the fighting rebels, but revolutions were notoriously made by comparatively small groups of determined armed men. According to the new doctrine this could not happen, if for no other reason because some communists would almost inevitably be mixed up in the revolution, or an alarmed government would allege they were. The President went on to say that the status quo was not sacred, but he had made it so. So far as the United States was concerned the method by which this nation was born was outlawed. There would be no more revolutions thereafter, in spite of the fact that many hundreds of millions of people lived a miserable existence under the misrule of a few. Revolution was finished. All of these peoples would have to stay put. If their rulers should decide to alleviate their condition somewhat, well and good, but they could not be coerced or subjected to "such subterfuges as political infiltration."

It is one thing to forbid revolution in a country where the democratic processes of peaceful change are fully established, and quite another to proscribe it where there is no democracy, or only a caricature of it. Instead of being loyal to his revolutionary heritage and welcoming democratic revolution wherever it might come, Truman spoke for the bulk of American conservatives and allied himself with reaction around the globe. This was not only morally wrong; it was blindness on a gigantic scale. For a century and a half it was our revolution, our new way of life, our example which moved the hearts and arms of men around the globe. For us now to declare that revolution was finished was to kill the American dream. It was to shut us out of the future at a time when a billion and a half people, nurtured in our revolutionary tradition, were determined to move upward into a better life. Instead of pitting democratic revolution against Red revolution, Truman presented to the communists the entire field of revolutionary activity and condemned his own people to the sterile and hopeless task of trying to prevent all forcible social change everywhere.

Fortunately there had to be an early retreat from this impossible position. In Indonesia we were soon to assist democratic revolution against Dutch imperialism, but the chief motive was still to save Indonesia from communism, not to give the islanders their just deserts. By placing us on the "anti" side, Truman conceded all dynamism to the Soviets and condemned his countrymen to a world-wide defense of the Western social order, including for many years the dying colonial empires.

Encirclement of the Soviet Union Proclaimed. The wheel had come to full circle with a vengeance. The isolationist United States, desiring only to be let alone, had become the world's policeman. Wherever public order was disturbed, we would be there. Wherever the Soviet Government or communism attempted an advance the United States would combat it. The most gigantic land power on the face of the globe, living on the opposite side of the earth from the United States, was to be fenced in at all points. Thus far and no farther! In the two previous balance of power struggles Germany had complained constantly that she was being encircled, but no one of her opponents ever dreamed of admitting that she was. Now Mr. Truman had proclaimed from one of the world's greatest rostrums the most gigantic encirclement ever conceived in the mind of man.

TRUMAN DOCTRINE ISSUES

1. *Why was the Doctrine promulgated at the start of the Moscow Conference of Foreign Ministers?*
This meeting had been scheduled months ahead to begin on March 10. It opened on that date and two days later the President delivered

his explosive message to Congress. Many people were puzzled by the simultaneity of these two events. Why did Truman choose the opening of the conference, which met to make a beginning on a treaty of peace for Germany, to explode his bomb shell? What to do about Germany was the next question to be decided, and the greatest. Did the President mean to torpedo the conference?

. . .Reports indicate fairly clearly that there was no hesitation about blanketing the conference with the Truman Doctrine. It was even expected that a dose of real toughness would bring hard-boiled Russian leaders to terms. If not, well and good, since the Administration did not attach much importance to the conference anyway.

In practice the opposite result was as certain as anything could be. Given their deep suspicions of the capitalist West the Russian attitude in the conference would inevitably stiffen. In Moscow, Howard K. Smith watched the Soviets change from an attitude of "some amicability to a stubborn resistance on every detailed point of discussion." The Russians concluded that Truman was preparing to solve the depression he had warned about by an armament program.

2. *Was the emergency in Greece serious enough to justify the crisis atmosphere created?*

Our leaders knew that the Royalist Greek Government was likely to disappear fairly soon, unless we continued the heavy backing which Britain had supplied. Yet the operation in prospect was not a tremendous one, when compared either to the costs of the war or to our current budget. Couldn't the burden have been accepted as one of the war's consequences without any great commotion? The Administration began to make headway in converting the rank and file, before the President went before Congress. The collapse of the Greek Government was not likely to occur on April 1. Its position was not that utterly hopeless. Actually it survived another two months with only the promise of further support, while the Congress was deliberating beyond its allotted time. The Congress, too, resented deeply the crisis treatment to which it was subjected, giving it no choice but to appropriate the money or damage irreparably our national prestige. A more normal procedure should have secured authority to take over in Greece, perhaps with the Turkish angle omitted.

More argument with the Congress might have been required, but there does not seem to have been any serious question of taking a milder course, for the reason that the President and his advisers wanted to seize the occasion to draw a line with Russia.

3. *Was it necessary to by-pass UN?*

The defenders of the Greek-Turkish policy maintained that it was, because the Russians would have vetoed the program. This would have been the case, however, only if a security or "threat to the peace" issue were before the Security Council. The veto did not apply in the Economic and Social Council, whose subsidiary Food and Agriculture Organization had already prepared exhaustive plans for reconstruction in Greece. . . .

It might have been somewhat vexatious to have had the program administered through the UN, but there would have been the enormous advantage of having the direct participation of third parties in the endeavour. The authority of UN might not alone have made civil war unnecessary, without the military aid part of the program since the rebellion was supported by Greece's neighbors, but UN management would have practically precluded the success of the rebels and might have provided guarantees of amnesty which would have brought the majority of them down out of the mountains.

Actually, of course, our Government did not desire to stabilize Greece through the UN, because it intended to achieve a stroke of power politics on its own, with the maximum of emphasis on the authority of the United States. There was regret that the UN had not been "related" in some way to the move, especially when it developed that the American people strongly disapproved of our unilateral action and demanded that the UN be not ignored. At this stage our Government did its best to "notify" the UN, and under the Republican leadership of Senator Vandenberg it went so far as to give the UN the power to end the program by a simple vote, which we would honor regardless of a veto by friend or foe. This gift of a vetoless veto to UN was made in a body in which our majority was overwhelming on any East-West issue and this paper concession did not lessen our ability to play the hand ourselves in Greece.

As the X article and the Truman message both demonstrated, we had no desire to bring in UN, because both documents ruled out negotiation and settlement as objectives and relied in the last analysis upon force, force to put down the Greek revolution and force to contain the Soviet Union indefinitely thereafter.

4. *Was a domestic political purpose incidentally involved?*

Stout defiance of a nation's chief rival has usually been good politics. There have been exceptions. The power of a government to influence public opinion is so great that even extreme appeasement could be made temporarily popular in Britain and France. But ringing defiance has raised the national hackles and won approval far more often, in democracies as well as authoritarian states.

President Truman was also under a special temptation to seize the anti-communist issue from the Republicans. The press of early 1947 contains many responsible estimates that the Republican cry against communism in the election of 1946, coupled with protests against the too soft Russian policy of the Roosevelt Administration and efforts to link the New Deal and the Democrats with communism, had won votes, probably enough to turn the election to the Republicans.

A leader as politically conscious as Harry Truman could not but be concerned about this development. On March 23, 1947, only a few days after the promulgation of the Truman Doctrine, he issued a sweeping order providing for the examination of the loyalty of all government employees, more than 2,000,000 of them. This step was taken to prevent a hostile Republican Congress from playing havoc with his Administration, by hunting for "communists" all through it, but it was also a defensive political move. On April 20, Marquis Childs wrote that after the order was issued President Truman was reported to have said: "Well, that should take the Communist smear off the Democratic party!"

The wholesale loyalty purge was a defensive move, but the Truman Doctrine had the effect of a sweeping political offensive inside the United States, and it is hardly likely that the President was unaware of this aspect of his action. The Republicans did not dare to charge partisan motivation, since the Doctrine had been combined with the Greek question in such a way as to pose the issue of national security and patriotism, but their chagrin was deep. By one bold all-embracing stroke Truman had made himself the world's leading anti-communist. He would fight its advance, either directly or by infiltration, everywhere on the globe, with money, with arms and with men if necessary. Nobody could go further than that, and because the Republicans had themselves fought communism so recently and so loudly they could do nothing but support the Truman Doctrine. What appeared to be a winning issue had been taken from their hands. . . .

5.Did the international political situation require the issuance of the Doctrine?

In Greece a political vacuum yawned ahead, and in Western Europe a much bigger one was already plainly discernible. Some action was essential if the danger that communism would fill these vacuums was to be averted. The obvious move was large scale economic aid, to enable these countries to recover from the rigors of the great winter and from the deeper damages of the war. Such aid was indispensable, if there was to be any real recovery. Its proffer, too, would have been tangible and weighty evidence that the United States did not mean to abandon Europe to its fate, as after World War I.

On the other hand, there was a good case for a ringing political pronouncement that would tell the European peoples that we were behind them, that we were coming to their aid. Did such a declaration have to be anti-communist and anti-Russian? Was it imperative that global political war be formally declared and joined?

It is difficult to believe that this was the case, even on the showing of the Kennan article, which saw no acute, urgent menace in Soviet communism. The Soviets had achieved great political success as a result of the war, and their achievement in consolidating their hold on East Europe, in spite of our protests, had deeply nettled our leaders. The communist parties were vigorously active in Italy and France, as Fifth Columns if we like. Yet they were only *fifth* columns. The other four columns were lacking, in the absence of great economic misery. Russia's satellites were helping the communist-led rebels in Greece, but Moscow gave no sign of throwing decisive strength into that struggle.

On the contrary, the Kremlin had been well satisfied with the world at the start of the year. The satellite treaties had from its standpoint been successfully concluded. From ours the terms were somewhat bitter, but settlements had been made. The Moscow conference was meeting to attempt to settle the real question, what to do with Germany. That would not be easy but it meant a lot to Russia as well as to us. The Russians were not likely to disrupt a major diplomatic conference, at which they were hosts, by any rash, aggressive moves in Western Europe, or in Greece. They were assuming the continuance of peace making so strongly that even after the Truman Doctrine had ended any chance of practical accomplishment at the Moscow conference the Russians went on discussing the issues in Germany, ignoring the world salvo of the Truman Doctrine. Near the close of the conference Stalin told Marshall that the Moscow discussions had been only "the first skirmishes and brushes of the reconnaissance forces" on the German question. "Differences had occurred in the past on other questions, and as a rule, after people had exhausted themselves in dispute, they then recognized the necessity of compromise." The Russians had amply proved that they were tough, long, hard bargainers, but they had no thought of abandoning diplomacy and risking their remaining lives and resources on political war.

It was the United States which did that.

The Moscow Conference. As the Moscow Conference adjourned, April 24, 1947, Sumner Welles wrote that it had run about in a vicious circle for six weeks. He urged the United States and the Soviet Union to reach a direct agreement upon the basis for an overall settlement. On the same day, Reston wrote that Washington was "in a black and cynical mood about the Moscow conference." On Capitol Hill there was nothing but "pessimistic resignation to an endless procession of relief and military appropriations."

On his way home Marshall said, April 25th, that East-West differences "have got to be reconciled," adding that "it is only a question how long it will take to do so." When Marshall had seen Stalin, on April 15, "the meeting was very much in the nature of a military 'briefing'" reported Joseph C. Harsch, the responsible Washington correspondent of the *Christian Science Monitor,* on April 29. The presentation of the Marshall brief took about thirty minutes. Stalin then made some comments and asked a few questions on specific points, "but there was nothing that could be called a discussion," or "an attempt to negotiate." The meeting was "most friendly" and Stalin was courteous to his guest.

In his radio report on the conference, published April 30, Dulles explained why Russia's demands on Germany could not be accepted by the United States, adding that we had not come home discouraged. This was not the viewpoint of Representative Charles A. Eaton, Chairman of the House Committee on Foreign Affairs, who told the House Rules Committee on April 29 that "two worlds are in head-on collision. One of them is going to survive." It was not difficult to persuade Eaton that this was true, but it is significant that he again posed the "either-or" choice the day after a secret White House conference, just as he had on emerging from the White House gathering on February 28. This horrendous choice was, of course, contained in the Truman Doctrine message when the President said, "nearly every nation must choose between alternative ways of life." No room was left for diversity, for many different kinds of systems. It must be one or the other.

6. *Did the military necessity of the United States justify our guardianship of the Turkish Straits?*

This is the most difficult aspect of the Truman Doctrine to assess. The geopolitical argument pushed to its logical conclusion justifies that part of the Truman Doctrine address which was frankly military.

The Soviets in control of Greece could outflank the Straits and dominate them. Then they could dominate Turkey and push on into the great oil fields of the Near East, through Iraq to Iran and down into Arabia. At this point they could control the land bridge between Europe and Asia and between Europe and Africa. They could also control the vital air routes in the same strategic area and end the freedom of the seas at Suez, the shortest sea route between the great populations of Europe and Asia. And everywhere they went their closed economic system could shut out our commerce, certainly our investments.

Then from Suez they could cross over into Africa, take North Africa away from the British and French, carry out social revolution everywhere and sweep down to Dakar, from which they could cross the narrow neck of the Atlantic to Brazil, conquer Catholic South America and come up to the Panama Canal, endangering that American waterway, so vital to our commerce. This is the kind of fatal progression which we feared from Hitler, rightly and deeply. . . .

If the Soviet Union was about to embark on this same raging imperial course, it was our bounden duty to prevent it. Yet the entire Kennan thesis, which rationalized the containment doctrine, denied that Russia was a threat of this character. On the contrary, she was tired, gravely wounded and full of inner contradictions of her own which would probably break her up. She was patient, would readily accept reverses, only needed persistent pushing back.

It is, of course, possible to reconcile these apparently contradictory lines of argument by saying that once in Greece the Russians would have infiltrated and advanced from the Dardanelles to Panama, by patient steps over a long period of time. Nevertheless, the two theories fairly well cancel each other. It would seem that we must choose one or the other as the basic justification for American control of the Turkish Straits. . . .

Is there any possible reconciliation between the long-term Western rights in the Straits and the right of the Russians to strategic security there? Given any normal confidence among the powers a solution would not be difficult. The Russians could be conceded their base at the Straits, or a genuine internationalization of this waterway could be worked out through the United Nations, to apply also to the Suez and Panama Canals. Our instinctive feeling about UN control of Panama is a measure of Russian feeling about the Straits. . . .

Sir Bernard Pares, English historian of Russia, assessed the long-term situation accurately when he wrote that the Truman Doctrine meant simply that the United States was taking over from England "the task of keeping Russia from the sea." This task had "nothing to do with Russian Communism." We could not offer friendship to a self respecting country on the principle: "We may do what we like, take what we like, but you may not. Freedom of the seas, yes, but not for you." This appraisal should give a fairly clear glimpse of Russian feeling about the Straits. . . .

It is essential to bear in mind, also, that we assumed the military guardianship of the Straits at a time when we had a monopoly of atomic weapons which precluded any overt Russian move, at the Straits or elsewhere, even if such a move had been contemplated.

7. *Was the Truman Doctrine a declaration of war?*

Formally and legally it was not. This could be asserted with a perfectly straight face, and with ample legal documentation. The Soviet Union was not mentioned, nor the Turkish Straits. We had a right to aid any friendly government that we wished to help. Turkey felt pressed and there was a crisis in Greece. We had as much right to proclaim an anti-communist crusade—or holding operation—as the Russian controlled press had to proclaim the inevitability of Western capitalism's collapse and the wickedness of Western "imperialism."

All this is incontrovertible and, given both our deep vexation over the communist organization of East Europe and the geopolitical argument, some action on our part in Greece was foreordained. Greece would not be allowed to fall into the Soviet orbit. Some anti-communist connotation was also advisable to secure quick congressional approval.

These considerations still leave the question whether it was wise and statesmanlike to issue a global declaration setting limits both to communist expansion and Soviet expansion. It can readily be argued that this was the straight-forward thing to do, to draw a line around both. Yet strategically it was a rash and unenforceable commitment. The Soviet Union already occupied the Heartland of Eurasia to its full limits, and all of our sea and air power, plus the A-bomb could not indefinitely prevent her from pushing out if she chose. Worse still, an open direct proclamation of encirclement was one of the best means of causing her to choose to push out.

The global containment Doctrine committed the United States to standing guard, not only at the Straits but all around the vast perimeter of the Soviet Union and its satellites. It pledged the prestige and resources of the United States, and especially the prestige of Mr. Truman, at virtually all points on the earth which mattered, either militarily or politically, leaving the initiative to the Russians and to local communist movements. Wherever either chose to fight we would accept the battlefield, no matter how remote or unfavorable. This was clearly a self-defeating policy, one fitted to squander our resources on the way to an immeasurable, unmanageable war.

Turning Point. The defenders of the Truman Doctrine announced with satisfaction that it was the end of an era, the period of "appeasement," and the beginning of a new era of firm containment. However, a full appraisal indicated that a much more fateful turn had been made, the turn from a post-war period to a pre-war atmosphere. The Truman Doctrine and the X article both ignored the problem of settling the Second World War, giving the impression that no settlement could be reached, that it was to be hereafter a matter of pressure and counter pressure. Less than two years after the bombs stopped falling in Europe American diplomacy came close to abdicating. Its arguing powers were exhausted. Stronger measures would have to be taken.

In this sense the Truman Doctrine was an effective declaration of war, one which had formed in Mr. Truman's mind in the autumn of 1945, almost before the fumes of Hiroshima had drifted around the earth. It gave notice to both sides, and to innumerable millions of people all over the world who wanted no fresh conflict, that a new global struggle was joined. It started trains of fear and hatred and action in many millions of minds, centering around Washington and Moscow, which ran for many years.

The judgment of James P. Warburg is likely to stand the test of history: that the Truman Doctrine message was "an ill-considered, unwise and ambiguous document," one calculated to arouse fear and aggressive hatreds" rather than to inform and persuade, one which opened a "Pandora's box of ugly emotions" in the breasts of "extreme Russia-haters, red-baiters and reactionaries of all sorts" and which brought the precariously balanced structure of peace to its moment of greatest jeopardy."

Two years later Gerald W. Johnson, an experienced editor and biographer, came to the same conclusion. He wrote of President Truman that "the most grievous of all his errors was enunciation of the Truman Doctrine that involved us in the Greek adventure and might have brought on far worse evils had it not been partially retrieved by the Marshall Plan."

Johnson added that in 1945 the moral hegemony of the world was within Truman's grasp, "but it has slipped from his fingers."

This is a measure of the loss involved in Truman's belligerence. It is easy enough to declare cold war, draw lines and hurl thunderbolts. It requires statesmanship to make peace and draw the nations nearer together.

Diplomacy is also required, an art which was almost forgotten after "we were captured by the illusion that the rivalry of nations can be regulated by public pronouncements, from which as a matter of prestige no one can recede, and the collision of irresistible forces with immovable objects."

There can be no real understanding of the Cold War unless chronology is kept in mind. What came first? What was action and what reaction? The later event could not be the cause of the earlier.

Especially is it necessary to consider what followed the Truman Doctrine. Not everything which came after it was an effect of the Doctrine, but its effects upon Soviet policy and action were bound to be profound.

There does not seem to be evidence of any sudden turn of Soviet policy to hostility toward the United States or toward the West after World War II. Frederick C. Barghoorn, a student of Soviet policy who works constantly with Russian language sources, speaks of "the gradual process by which the Politburo openly reverted to its pre-war line, and transferred the symbols of 'reaction,' 'aggression,' and 'imperialism' from Germany and Japan to Britain and America."

The first evidence of such transference which Barghoorn cites was the speech of President Kalinin to Communist Party secretaries in which he asked them to "speak frankly" to the collective farmers about the dangers to "our state structure and social order" still remaining after the elimination of Nazi Germany, which he characterized as "only the most immediate" danger. Then Stalin in his famous election speech of February 9, 1946 boasted of the triumphant survival of the Soviet system in World War II, a war that he ascribed to "the inevitable result of the development of world economic and political forces on the basis of modern monopolistic capitalism," which was incapable "under present capitalist conditions" of peacefully adjusting the conflicts which lead to war.

The admonition by Kalinin hardly seems sensational, as of August

1945, after Truman's verbal assault on Molotov in the White House on April 23, 1945; after the bitter controversy over Poland and East Europe which followed; after the frictions at the San Francisco conference, the outburst of preventive war talk against Russia in the United States and the sharp turn of the Truman Administration away from the Roosevelt policy of working with Russia—not to speak of the great impact of the Hiroshima A-bomb in Moscow. Nor does Stalin's February 1946 reassertion of communist dogma about the relation between monopolistic capitalism and war seem extraordinary.

It was not until Andrei Zhdanov's speech of September 1947 that a post-war division of the world into two camps was proclaimed in Russia, "the anti-democratic and imperialist camp on the one side, and the anti-imperialist and democratic on the other." Attacking the Marshall Plan as a device for "the enslavement of Europe," Zhdanov accused the United States of seeking world domination. Because her "monopolists" feared the success of communism they had launched a world-wide crusade against communism, he charged.

This was undoubtedly political warfare, but it can hardly be considered remarkable after the enunciation of the Truman Doctrine, Kennan's elaboration of the American containment drive and the Marshall Plan—altogether the greatest peace time political-economic offensive on record. An offensive of this character was bound to bring replies, both ideological and actual.

LLOYD C. GARDNER
Architects of Illusion

SOMETIME IN MAY 1944 the new Secretary of the Navy James V. Forrestal exclaimed to a friend, "My God . . . you and I and Bill Bullitt are the only ones around the President who know the Russian leaders for what they are." Forrestal thought his doubts about the "Grand Alliance" set him apart from most of official Washington. Preoccupied with his own fears about the shape of postwar politics at home and abroad, he mistook the public rhetoric of the Office of War Information for the private views of Roosevelt's advisers. . . .

. . .Contemptuous of theoreticians, intellectual "meddlers," and social planners who criticized capitalism, Forrestal nonetheless chose the most ideological and theological among alternative explanations of Russian attitudes and motivations. A conservative Democrat who had been called to Washington after a spectacular rise to power and fortune on Wall Street, he was extremely uncomfortable around "New Dealers." Even more than other conservatives, Forrestal thought world capitalism was under seige, and throughout the war he kept large files on individuals, organizations, and publications he suspected of being under communist influence. The Navy Secretary believed that the New Dealers rejoiced at Labour's victory in the British elections of July 1945 because it represented what they wanted to see happen in America, and because now they could promote socialism throughout the world directly by underwriting a Labour government with American tax dollars. . . .

. . . During Cabinet debates on atomic policy the following September, Forrestal argued that it would be dangerous to enter into atomic control agreements with the Russians because, like the Japanese, they were essentially "oriental" in their thinking. Such value judgments were also at the heart of his profound conviction that East-West disputes, now Russian-American conflicts, were basically ideological. His deepest worry was that the President and

---

Mr. Gardner is Professor of History at Rutgers University.

his advisers did not grasp these facts, that they did not understand the United States was grappling for its soul with a spiritual power working its temporal will through the Red Army. In this state of anxiety, Forrestal kept searching for the one complete document, the one perfect explanation of the sources of Soviet con-duct. . . . Forrestal's emotional obsession was a parody of the old fear that European radicalism would finally terrorize the world as a German head on a Russian peasant. Forrestal made it out as a German head on a Mongol warrior.

As parody on parody, Forrestal's demeanor resembled Ichabod Crane's terrified flight in Sleepy Hollow—were it not for the fact that these views soon were not considered unusual at all. In a letter to Walter Lippmann, Forrestal insisted that the fundamental ques-tion was whether the United States had to deal with a nation or a religion—but he added that religion, after all, was merely the practical extension of philosophy. . . ."A lot of admittedly brainy men believe that governments, history, science and business can be rationalized into a state of perfection," he said in 1947. "Their ideals all come out of the same hat whether it is one worn by a German, a Russian or a Stafford Cripps!"

Having ruled out all theorists of radical social change as charla-tans of roughly equal talents and the forebears of tyrannical despots, Forrestal returned again and again to the pragmatic evolution of the American social-economic-fiscal system, which, he wrote Moley, had produced the major contribution to man's welfare in the twentieth century—the creation of the managerial class. Despite the admiration of some of the nation's thinkers for foreign ideology, he added, American capitalism was still the chief prop for the rest of the world. "Our present position in the world," he suggested to the dean of the Harvard Graduate School, "is that we are trying to provide the catalyst for recovery against almost insuperable difficulties in the way of inertia and the disposition to try new schemes of social and political organization which, tried after the last war, produced Hitler and Stalin."

The economic problem was an international problem because the United States could not act dictatorially if it were to fall into depression; yet such a depression was inevitable unless world order was re-established, which meant above all else restoration of commerce, business, and international trade. . . .

By June 1946 Forrestal had found George Kennan, whose views on Soviet behavior, according to the editors of his published diaries, provided the "whole truth" about Russia that Forrestal had been seeking since the end of the war. In another year Kennan would himself become famous as the "secret" author of an anonymous article by "Mr. X" in the July 1947 *Foreign Affairs*—"The Sources of Soviet Conduct. . . ."

This anonymity disappeared almost at once, and the article Kennan thought no more about propelled him to the front rank of Cold War policy-makers. Even before it appeared in print, Kennan had been named to head Secretary Marshall's new State Department Policy Planning Staff. He moved to that position from the National War College, where he had been serving as Deputy for Foreign Affairs. Both appointments owed much to Forrestal's personal intervention. Never close to Roosevelt or to Truman, he sought to bolster his advice to those Presidents by seeing to it that views congenial to his reached the most important private decision-makers of American foreign policy. . . .

Before going into the results of the Forrestal-Kennan "collaboration," the "X" article itself, a few words are needed on the terms "realistic" and "realist.". . . The simplest way to define "realism" might be to say that it was a reaction against the Wilsonian-Rooseveltian "idealism," particularly as expressed in "one-world-ism." The realists rejected much of the so-called traditional American approach to foreign policy in favor of European power-oriented approaches because America's excessive concern with moralism had resulted in a baleful neglect of the national interest and quixotic crusades to right the world's wrongs.

In Kennan's case, however, as in many others, this definition is not enough. Almost paradoxically, the realists of the early Cold War period became especially involved in an "idealism" of a different sort, one, however, that was surprisingly "Wilsonian" as well. "What was disturbing about the new realists of the forties and fifties," asserts intellectual historian Christopher Lasch, "was their willingness prematurely to commit themselves to a view of American society in which the United States appeared unambiguously as the leader of the 'free world' and the only alternative, for all its faults, to Soviet 'despotism.' "

The Forrestal-Kennan collaboration is fascinating for other reasons as well. Forrestal's conservatism came from his station in American life; Kennan, like Henry James, was almost completely alienated from that society. He returned from the American Embassy in Moscow in the 1930's, but the experience "only emphasized the degree of my estrangement." Like James he never grappled with the facts of American life, nor confronted the political-economic issues Forrestal faced daily. Kennan sought to evade the physical consequences of the "X" article almost at once, as James sought to avoid the physical in his fiction. For example, Kennan excluded military aid for Turkey; but Forrestal found in Kennan's writings precisely the justification he had been seeking to extend American naval power throughout the Mediterranean.

In Kennan's later writings it became clear that he always preferred a spheres-of-influence approach to the Soviet Union—albeit one heavily larded with moral condemnation of what the Russians were doing in their sphere—to the universalism of some of his "realist" colleagues in the State Department. Though Kennan was and is a consistent critic of the American world-view, the "X" article was used by Dean Acheson and others to justify the "holy pretense," and to exclude moral considerations when dealing with the barbarians. Therein, of course, lies much of the fascination with the article and its author, a fascination now shared by Kennan himself, as he reveals in his *Memoirs . . . .*

. . . The "X" article and the containment policy it described were taken over by other principals who were more sure of their roles and less concerned with the nuances and skills of the international drama. Some of the most important players went on to write their own versions of the policy. . . .

The "X" article acted as a powerful magnet on loose fragments of an ideology and shaped them into a pattern which was easily understood by men like Forrestal. These ideas were then transmitted to policy-makers generally, and ultimately into action. The State Department committee apparently viewed the "X" signature as a perfect symbol for the new policy formulation; symbols often become as important as substance in doctrinal matters. . . .

"In writing the X-article," Kennan says in his *Memoirs,* "I had in mind a long series of what seemed to me to be concessions, that we had made, during the course of the war and just after it, to Russian expansionist tendencies—concessions made in the hope and belief that they would promote collaboration between our government and the Soviet government in the postwar period." Perceiving that others now saw the failure of this policy, Kennan argues that he was concerned that Americans not jump to the panicky conclusion that war between the two super-powers was inevitable. Like Bullitt and Forrestal, he was dismayed by Roosevelt's faith in personal diplomacy; and he saw the proposed United Nations as a product of the longstanding American dream of projecting onto the world at large its national consensus and belief in juridical settlements of international disputes.

In George Frost Kennan the Presbyterian elder wrestled with the Bismarckian geopolitician: that struggle produced the "X" article. . . . This approach to the "X" article had three sources: his life-long convictions about human nature; a career-long belief that America had made too many concessions to the Soviets (and others) in the vain hope that a League of Nations would restrain man's inherent traits; and a more recent vexation, widely shared in official Washington, at Henry Wallace's plea for greater "trust" in Soviet-American relations.

Kennan interpreted Wallace's criticisms of the "get-tough" policy as a foolish desire to continue Rooseveltian personal diplomacy and, at Yale University, on October 1, 1946, indirectly criticized him in a lecture on the dangers of misunderstanding Soviet motives and policy. Unhappily, Kennan began, such bids for "trust" in international relations all too often had great appeal "to the Rotarian heart." But the Russian challenge demanded something more from Americans than "a few propitiatory offerings fearfully and hastily tossed in the path of the advancing opposition." It was important to disabuse ourselves completely of such feelings by employing the most dispassionate arguments and logic. Here again, however, Kennan's overreaction to Rooseveltian foreign policy led him to draw militant images for instructional purposes rather than describe the reality of Soviet capabilities. He was chasing Roosevelt's ghost in Henry Wallace. . . .

Some listeners, Kennan said, might find this analysis too ideological. "Never forget that ideology is the only positive feature in a regime which has otherwise brought little but harshness, cruelty and physical misery to the human beings who have fallen within the range of its influence." Ideology was the figleaf of Soviet respectability. Tear it away and all that was left was the last in a series of rulers "who have driven a great people from one military ordeal to another throughout the course of centuries in order to assure the security of their own oppressive regimes."

The destruction of Russia's two great enemies, Germany and Japan, had confronted these men with the horrible possibility that they might be forced to live in a friendly world. "Is it any wonder that they rose up as a body to deny that this precariousness had passed?" The Russians had only themselves to fear and only their backwardness to blame for their insecurity. Appeasement of these fears would not dispel Soviet ideology and could lead only down a path to which there was "no end short of the capitulation of the United States as a great power in the world and as the guardian of its own security."

> We can contribute only by a long-term policy of firmness, patience and understanding, designed to keep the Russians confronted with superior strength at every juncture where they might otherwise be inclined to encroach upon the vital interests of a stable and peaceful world, but to do this in so friendly and unprovocative a manner that its basic purposes will not be subject to misinterpretation.

The ratio between logic and conviction was changing, and the imagery had hardened; almost completely bypassed were the specific events which had led to the beginnings of Cold War or to the split in the Truman Cabinet which had produced Wallace's Madison Square Garden speech. It was all psychology and ideology. In this mood Kennan wrote what eventually became the "X" article for Secretary Forrestal. . . .

As in the Yale lecture on Wallace's Rotarian-like errors, Kennan placed his real emphasis on American behavior in meeting the Soviet challenge, not on the reality of that challenge itself. In formulating his containment policy, however, it was difficult for him to maintain any balance between reason and principle or political and military tactics. There was simply *no* clear delineation between such internal elements—just as real geographical limitations and boundaries break down when policy is applied. Containment could not be restricted to the five "key" regions, to political tactics, or to nondoctrinaire applications. Argument from moral conviction, especially in the new atomic age, guaranteed the absolutist character of the competition, while discussion of the techniques of this new struggle reciprocally reinforced this absolutism.

The first sentence of the "X" article, completed a few months later, went a long way to justify such a conclusion. Perhaps the nature of Forrestal's specific assignment had been just enough to tip Kennan's balance in favor of principle and military imagery: "The political personality of Soviet power, as we know it today, is the product of ideology and circumstances: ideology inherited by the present Soviet leaders from the movement in which they had their political origin, and circumstances *of the power* which they now have exercised for nearly three decades in Russia." Those circumstances, let us note, were not of Russia's international position in those three decades, but of the power which the Soviet leaders had exercised at home. It was a crucial definition and a crucial distinction. It made Kennan the original popularizer of the so-called "domestic change" thesis as well as the containment thesis. Its supporters have regarded diplomatic adjustment with the Soviets difficult if not impossible until there has been a "domestic change" inside Russia. The persistence of this theme in Kennan's writings even after he had abandoned containment in favor of "disengagement" further illustrates how difficult it was for him to separate his moral judgments from policy recommendations, at least so others could adopt a "realistic" policy. . . .

. . .Kennan did not mention America's part in the 1918–1920 intervention against the new Soviet regime, or Western efforts to keep Russia quarantined politically and morally throughout the following decade. As for collective security in the 1930's, Kennan said, there could never have been a time when Moscow regarded its relations with capitalist nations as based upon any mutual interest. Instead, Soviet motives remained implacable behind the changing face of its diplomacy. Whenever that face changed expression, however slight the movement, there would always be foolish Americans eager to rush in and claim that Russian goals had changed—even to take credit for bringing about these marvelous alterations. With this final shot at World War II diplomacy, Kennan moved on to his most famous image, that of the whole Soviet governmental machine moving inexorably along a prescribed path, "like a persistent toy automobile wound up and headed in a given direction, stopping only when it meets with some unanswerable force." But the United States, he concluded, had the power to increase enormously the strains under which Soviet power must operate, and to force upon the Kremlin a far greater degree of moderation and circumspection that it had had to observe in recent years—"and in this way to promote tendencies which must eventually find their outlet in either the break-up or the gradual mellowing of Soviet power. For no mystical, Messianic movement—and particularly not that of the Kremlin—can face frustration indefinitely without eventually adjusting itself in one way or another to the logic of that state of affairs."

The "X" article "soon became the center of a veritable whirlpool of publicity," Kennan said with remembered feelings of alarm in his *Memoirs.* Both *Life* and the *Reader's Digest* printed long excerpts from it, and the single word "containment" was used as a concise description of American foreign policy—even by those who had never read the "book." John Foster Dulles boldly sought to hang on it all the faults of the Truman administration's foreign policy in the plank he wrote for the 1952 Republican platform: "We shall again make liberty into a beacon light of hope that will penetrate the dark places. It will mark the end of the negative, futile and immoral policy of 'containment' which abandons countless human beings to a despotism and godless terrorism, which in turn enables the rulers to forge the captives into a weapon of our destruction."

When the chance came to intervene for "liberty" in the 1956 Hungarian revolution, even Dulles preferred to stay in the dark with containment rather than risk a nuclear confrontation with Moscow. By that time, Kennan had shifted to a new formulation, "disengagement." With the success of the Marshall Plan seemingly assured, Kennan had begun the search for a way to allow the Soviet Union to disengage itself from its military presence in Eastern and Central

Europe. The explosion of the Russian atomic bomb in September 1949 speeded this thought process. But Secretary Acheson was not yet ready to negotiate. So long as there was the possibility of a major technological breakthrough, the Cold War might yet be won. At least one could hold out that hope a while longer. Of course, after hydrogen bombs came intercontinental ballistic missiles, and then a series of imagined "gaps."

This search for a perfect negotiating position, as Kennan realized, denied the desirability or even the possibility of significant diplomatic adjustments, including disengagement. But his new prophecy was not wanted in the temple built to containment, and the founder of the faith was driven from its walls as a "mystic" heretic.

The highly ideological formulation of the containment thesis foretold such a result. Kennan was himself alarmed when he read Walter Lippmann's perceptive critique of the "X" article and the Truman Doctrine. In a series of daily newspaper columns, later published as *The Cold War: A Study in U.S. Foreign Policy,* Lippmann set about wrecking the containment thesis from its ideological underpinnings to its tactical prescriptions for checking the Soviets. Soviet foreign policy was the same as Russian foreign policy under Peter the Great, Lippmann countered. Ideologies might come and go, but Russian national interests (like those of the British Empire) were eternal. Containment gave an opponent shorter logistical lines of communication; it saddled the U.S. with unreliable allies to hold the line; it meant, in sum, trying to police the world. While Kennan had in fact taken many of Lippmann's positions in the intra-administration debates on the Truman Doctrine and the Marshall Plan, in the "X" article he was preoccupied with the irony of man's nature and destiny as he perceived it in the grotesque and misshapen figure of Stalinist "Marxism." Kennan and his later followers all too often dispensed with any historical analysis except that which sustained their particular ironic view. . . .

If, as now seems reasonable given Kennan's explanations in his *Memoirs* and his penetrating critiques of the liberal world-view in *American Foreign Policy, 1900–1950,* he had set out only to instruct American policy-makers, not to start a crusade, he did himself and his purposes a grave disservice in the "X" article. Always standing behind "Mr. X" was Forrestal, the man who had given him the time and opportunity to perform a special function for the American policy-making community. A profoundly moral man whose revulsion at the excesses and inhumanities carried out in the name of social justice overrode nearly all his other feelings and ultimately led him into equally profound disagreement with his nation's foreign policies in the 1960's, Kennan watched with increasing dismay as the "X" article assumed the attributes and separate life of an anonymous spokesman for American foreign policy, one whose pen sounded the call to arms in the early morning of the Cold War.

III The Cold War in Perspective

In this section, Herz, in succinct question and answer form, simply recapitulates the sequence of crucial events and decisions bearing on the origins of the cold war. He employs a minimum of personal judgment, preferring to let the facts speak for themselves. In the round-table discussion, a group of European and American scholars return to the broader problem of the nature of the conflict and the difficulties involved in probing the essence of the matter. Finally, Maier and LaFeber seek to analyze the dispute among historians. Maier is critical of some of the main lines of the revisionist attack, while LaFeber accepts much of the validity of the newer writing. Both, however, are concerned with going beyond academic disputation by raising the whole controversy to a broader intellectual plane.

14 The Cold War in Perspective

M. HERZ
The Beginnings of the Cold War

QUESTIONS AND ANSWERS

QUESTION 1: When the United States and Great Britain defined their war aims in the Atlantic Charter, was the United States at war? ANSWER: No. The Atlantic Charter was signed on August 14, 1941. The United States entered the war on December 7, 1941.

QUESTION 2: Was Russia, which was at war at the time, consulted about this definition of aims? ANSWER: No, Russia was not consulted when the Atlantic Charter was drafted, but it was subsequently asked to adhere.

QUESTION 3: What was the British understanding of the applicability of the Atlantic Charter? ANSWER: Churchill specifically declared that it did not apply to the British Empire.

QUESTION 4: When the Soviet Union subscribed to the Atlantic Charter, did it do so without reservation? ANSWER: No. The Soviets entered a reservation that "the practical application of these principles" should be adapted to the "circumstances, needs, and historic peculiarities of particular countries."

QUESTION 5: Did this qualified acceptance of the Atlantic Charter mean that they foreswore the idea of spheres of influence in Europe? ANSWER: No. From the beginning the Russians attempted to get acknowledgment of a privileged position in eastern Europe, for which they were willing in return to acknowledge a privileged British position in western Europe.

QUESTION 6: Was Britain prepared to accept the initial Soviet war aims to the effect that Russia should regain all the territories it had gained as a result of the Nazi-Soviet Pact of 1939? ANSWER: Yes. Churchill considered that this "was the basis on which Russia acceded to the [Atlantic] Charter."

QUESTION 7: Why did Britain not give these assurances to the Soviet Union? ANSWER: Because of U.S. objections to any ter-

---

Mr. Herz is a member of the United States Foreign Service.

From *The Beginnings of the Cold War* by M. Herz. Copyright © 1966 by Indiana University Press. Reprinted by permission of the publisher.

ritorial settlement prior to the peace conference. Also, in the U.S. view, such a settlement would not have been in accordance with point two of the Atlantic Charter.

QUESTION 8: After Russia was attacked by Germany in 1941, was the Polish government-in-exile prepared to enter into friendly relations with the Soviet Union? ANSWER: Yes, but only on condition that Russia renounce her war aims and reestablish the Polish state in its pre-1939 boundaries.

QUESTION 9: Did Russia show any willingness to consider these terms for cooperation with the Polish government-in-exile? AN-SWER: No, not even at a time when the Russians were most sorely beset by the invading German armies.

QUESTION 10: What brought about the break between the Soviet Union and the Polish government-in-exile? ANSWER: The discovery by the Germans of the bodies of murdered Polish officers, which led the Poles in London to call for an investigation by the International Red Cross.

QUESTION 11: What was Churchill's reaction to the Polish call for a Red Cross investigation? ANSWER: He thought it a mistake. He said to the premier of the Polish exile government: "If they are dead nothing you can do will bring them back."

QUESTION 12: What was the opinion of George Kennan on the action of the Polish government-in-exile which brought the break with the Soviet Union? ANSWER: "It is hard, in retrospect, to see how the Poles could have done less."

QUESTION 13: On the basis of all the evidence that has become available since that time, does it look as if the story about the Katyn massacre was a Nazi provocation? ANSWER: The weight of evidence is that the Polish officers in question were killed by the Russians, but there is reason to believe that this was the result of a mistake.

QUESTION 14: What, subsequently, was the principal obstacle to reestablishment of relations between the Soviet Union and the Polish government-in-exile? ANSWER: The question of Poland's eastern border. Neither the Soviets nor the Polish exiles were willing to accept, or even discuss, the view of the other side on this question.

QUESTION 15: What was the position of the London Poles with respect to the impending entry into Poland of Russian troops as they were driving the Germans back toward Germany? ANSWER: They threatened to call upon the Polish underground to resist the Russians if they advanced into Poland without a prior agreement with the government-in-exile.

QUESTION 16: What did Russia next propose with respect to the postwar frontiers of Poland? ANSWER: At the Tehran Conference, Stalin proposed that in return for acceptance of the eastern borders of 1939, Poland should be compensated by getting German territory up to the Oder River.

QUESTION 17: What was the American reaction to this proposal? ANSWER: There was no official American reaction to this proposal at the Conference. But Roosevelt privately explained to Stalin that he was worried about the reaction of Americans of Polish extraction.

QUESTION 18: What was the British reaction to this proposal? ANSWER: Churchill agreed with it in general terms, subject to some modifications of Poland's eastern frontier in favor of Poland.

QUESTION 19: How did Churchill attempt to persuade the Polish exile government to accept this new territorial arrangement? AN-SWER: He repeatedly urged it upon Mikolajczyk. He said that if the exiles did not act quickly, he "could not be responsible for anything that might take place."

QUESTION 20: By the time the Russians reached the old Polish frontier, would they have been satisfied with an agreement on the territorial question? ANSWER: No, by this time they had started to talk about the need for a "friendly" (i.e., Communist-dominated) Polish government.

QUESTION 21: By the time the Russian forces were in territory which Russia itself recognized as Polish, what was the Russian position? ANSWER: It had hardened further. Now the Russians asked not only for acceptance of their territorial position, but they set up a puppet organization, the so-called Lublin Committee, which they said must furnish the majority of any Polish government.

QUESTION 22: Why did the U.S. government not take a vigorous and clear-cut position on these issues at that time? ANSWER: Because, as Roosevelt had stated, he was concerned about the

Polish-American vote in the 1944 elections; and also, as Hull stated later, because the United States needed Russian military cooperation in view of the forthcoming invasion of western Europe.

QUESTION 23: Who were the leaders of the Polish uprising against the Germans in Warsaw, which the Russians refused to support? ANSWER: They were exponents of the government-in-exile.

QUESTION 24: What is McNeill's opinion about the failure to resolve the Polish question at that time? ANSWER: "The failure of Allied policy to achieve a peaceable settlement of the Polish problem in the first seven months of 1944 may well be considered the turning-point in the history of the Grand Alliance."

QUESTION 25: Who was in control of Poland at the time of the Yalta Conference? ANSWER: The Red Army had occupied almost all of prewar Poland.

QUESTION 26: What was agreed at Yalta with respect to Poland's frontiers? ANSWER: While the United States did not agree on the western frontiers, the eastern frontier was in effect settled substantially along the lines of the original Russian position.

QUESTION 27: What did the West get out of this belated acceptance of the Soviet position on its western border? ANSWER: Nothing. But some Western participants apparently thought that they had obtained Russian agreement to a democratic rump Poland.

QUESTION 28: How about the famous Declaration on Liberated Europe? Was this not a quid pro quo for acceptance of the Soviet border proposal? ANSWER: It was hardly discussed at Yalta and the operative clause was watered down by the Russians so that it provided only for "mutual consultation" instead of the "machinery for the carrying out of the joint responsibilities" which the United States had proposed. However, the United States attached great importance to the principles laid down in that document. (See also Questions 55 and 56).

QUESTION 29: What was agreed at Yalta with respect to the Polish government? ANSWER: It was agreed that the existing (Communist) government would be "reorganized" into a new, fully representative government and that that government should be "pledged to the holding of free and unfettered elections."

QUESTION 30: What was the Russian interpretation of this

agreement? ANSWER: It was that only Poles who had agreed to the Yalta territorial decisions could participate in the reorganized government, and that only a few non-Communist Poles could be included in the provisional government.

QUESTION 31: In the ensuing arguments between the Western Allies and Russia, what was the Western position? ANSWER: That the Yalta Agreement called for a completely new Polish government and that a veto on some prospective participants violated the very foundation of the Yalta Agreement.

QUESTION 32: What was Roosevelt's personal view about the position? ANSWER: He had doubts about it, at least on one occasion. As he wrote Churchill, he was aware that under the Yalta agreement "somewhat more emphasis" would be placed on the Lublin (Communist) Poles.

QUESTION 33: Did the Polish exile leaders agree with the Western position on this matter? ANSWER: Not entirely. Some of them actually felt, like the Russians, that the Yalta Agreement had in effect conceded that the new Polish government would be dominated by the Communists.

QUESTION 34: What was President Truman's position on this matter? ANSWER: It was that the Russians were violating the Yalta Agreement and that the agreement could not be interpreted as involving the establishment of a Communist-dominated provisional Polish government.

QUESTION 35: What was the Russian reaction to this position? ANSWER: It was that it amounted to "abrogation" of the Yalta decisions.

QUESTION 36: How did the Hopkins mission contribute to a solution of this issue? ANSWER: It opened the way for the eventual establishment of a Communist-dominated provisional Polish government.

QUESTION 37: Did the Russians live up to their obligation to cause "free and unfettered elections" to be held in Poland? ANSWER: No. Elections were held only in 1947, after the non-Communist parties had been thoroughly terrorized.

QUESTION 38: What was the American position on spheres of influence in Europe? ANSWER: The United States was strongly opposed to them. Secretary of State Hull stated that he felt that Russia's security could be better guaranteed by a "strong postwar peace organization."

QUESTION 39: What was the first country liberated or occupied by the Allies (then called United Nations) in the war? ANSWER: Italy, whose surrender was accepted "by authority of the Governments of the United States and Great Britain and in the interest of the United Nations."

QUESTION 40: What was the Russian position on their role in the political direction of the occupation of Italy? ANSWER: They wanted a full role in it.

QUESTION 41: What was the U.S.-British response to this? ANSWER: The request was very poorly received, and the Russians were excluded from the Control Commission. When an "Inter-Allied Advisory Council" was later established, it had no role in determining occupation policies.

QUESTION 42: Did this not imply that the Western Allies in fact viewed the territories conquered or liberated by them as an exclusive sphere of influence? ANSWER: Yes, at least as far as the wartime period was concerned, but there is no evidence that this was ever explicitly stated as policy.

QUESTION 43: What was the reason for this Western position? ANSWER: The United States and Britain did not wish the Russians to have a role in the occupation of Italy because they were worried that the Russians would support the activities of the Italian Communists; and there is good evidence that that worry was justified.

QUESTION 44: When the United States and Britain later demanded a share in determining occupation policies in Rumania, what was the Russian reaction? ANSWER: The Russians refused, referring to Italy as a precedent.

QUESTION 45: What was the real Russian reason? ANSWER: There is no evidence for this, but quite probably they were afraid that the United States and Britain would support the activities of the anti-Communists.

QUESTION 46: What, then, was the difference between the situation in Italy and in Rumania? ANSWER: In Italy, the Western Allies were pretty sure that in free elections the anti-Communists, whom they favored, would win. In Rumania, the Russians had good reason to fear that in free elections the Communists, whom they favored, would lose.

QUESTION 47: How did the Russians in fact use their predominance in occupied Rumania? ANSWER: They forced a Communist-dominated government on King Michael.

QUESTION 48: When Churchill was prepared, early in 1944, to recognize Russian ("temporary") predominance in Rumania in return for their recognition of similar British predominance in Greece, what was the American reaction? ANSWER: The United States spiked the deal on the ground that it would conflict with the basic declarations of postwar aims and would create a dangerous precedent.

QUESTION 49: When Churchill finally in October 1944 made an agreement with Stalin that in effect established spheres of influence in the Balkans, what was the American reaction? ANSWER: The United States acquiesced in the deal but four months later, at Yalta, it was nullified by the Declaration on Liberated Europe which substituted broad general principles for the pragmatic and temporary arrangement between Churchill and Stalin.

QUESTION 50: What was the immediate effect of the spheres-of-influence arrangement on the British position in Greece? ANSWER: It was most favorable, and Churchill subsequently (at Yalta) expressed his thanks to Stalin for "not having taken too great an interest in Greek affairs."

QUESTION 51: What was the effect of the Churchill-Stalin agreement on the situation in Yugoslavia? ANSWER: Britain and Russia jointly tried to create a coalition government. Stalin encouraged Churchill to move British troops into northwestern Yugoslavia.

QUESTION 52: What was Tito's position with regard to a British military operation in Yugoslavia? ANSWER: He was violently opposed to it. This did not, however, prevent the Russians from reiterating their proposal three months later, at the Yalta Conference.

QUESTION 53: Did the Churchill-Stalin agreement in fact result in a 50:50 division of influence in Yugoslavia? ANSWER: It did not, and Churchill complained about this, albeit rather weakly.

QUESTION 54: What credence should be given to Stalin's statement at Yalta that he had little influence on Tito? ANSWER: From evidence that has become available after Yugoslavia defected from the Soviet bloc, it appears that Tito in any case strongly resented the Churchill-Stalin agreement.

QUESTION 55: Was the Declaration on Liberated Europe which was signed at Yalta put into effect by the Russians? ANSWER: No. The principles of joint assistance to the people of the European liberated states or former Axis satellites, especially as regards the formation of "broadly representative governments" and the facilitating of free elections, were largely ignored.

QUESTION 56: In the opinion of the signatories, did the Declaration on Liberated Europe extinguish the spheres-of-influence deal which Churchill and Stalin had concluded in October 1944? ANSWER: As far as the United States is concerned, the answer is clearly in the affirmative; but we cannot be sure that the Russians felt the same way. The anomalous situation in Hungary after Yalta suggests that the spirit of the October 1944 deal may have lingered on for quite some time.

QUESTION 57: In what respects was the situation in Hungary (where Churchill and Stalin had agreed on a 50:50 division of influence) "anomalous"? ANSWER: Hungary is the only Russian-occupied country where relatively free elections, resulting in a non-Communist majority, were permitted in 1945. (The Soviet-occupied zone of Austria was another such situation.)

QUESTION 58: But was not Hungary taken over by the Communists with Russian military support? ANSWER: Yes, but this took place only in 1947, long after the Cold War had begun. In 1945, the Russians had apparently not yet made up their mind on this matter. Perhaps they might then have been amenable to some bargaining, but this was never explored.

QUESTION 59: What did the United States have available for such bargaining? How about the threat of force? ANSWER: Roosevelt at Yalta said he did not believe American troops would stay in Europe much more than two years after the war.

QUESTION 60: What other bargaining counter might the United States have used in order to exercise a mitigating role at least in such countries as Hungary, Czechoslovakia, and Austria, where Russian predominance had not been accepted by Churchill? ANSWER:

Credits, in which the Russians were very interested in view of the devastation they had suffered in the war.

QUESTION 61: Did the Russians have reason to expect that American goods would be available to them on favorable terms after the war? ANSWER: Yes. There was much talk about the expected great American postwar "surplus." The chairman of the U.S. War Production Board and the president of the U.S. Chamber of Commerce ventilated the idea of large postwar credits in their talks with Russian leaders.

QUESTION 62: What was the approximate value of the U.S. "Lend-Lease" aid to Russia during the war? ANSWER: Nine and one-half billion dollars.

QUESTION 63: How was this aid used as leverage during the delicate negotiations with the Russians at the end of the war? ANSWER: It was not used at all. The aid was suddenly cut off in a manner which President Truman (who later rescinded the order) described as one that "made it appear as if somebody had been deliberately snubbed."

QUESTION 64: During the period immediately prior to the Yalta Conference, did Russia apply for a loan for postwar reconstruction? ANSWER: Yes, on January 3, 1945, Russia formally asked for a six billion dollar loan at $2^{1}/_{4}$ per cent interest.

QUESTION 65: Is there evidence that Roosevelt intended to use economic aid as a diplomatic instrument in his negotiations with Stalin? ANSWER: Yes, but it is not conclusive. Apparently he intended to discuss the matter at Yalta. Also, there is a memorandum in which Roosevelt noted that the Russians "in their occupied territories will do more or less what they wish" and went on to say that he did not intend to "break off or delay negotiations" over future Lend-Lease deliveries.

QUESTION 66: Was either the future of Lend-Lease or the Russian request for a six-billion-dollar credit actually used for bargaining purposes at the Yalta Conference? ANSWER: No. Neither of these two matters came up between Roosevelt and Stalin during any of their discussions at Yalta, where the greatest amount of time had to be devoted to Poland.

QUESTION 67: In what other way did the Russians attempt to lay their hands on substantial amounts of capital to help in their reconstruction? ANSWER: Through German reparations, which they wished to fix at $20 billion at Yalta, with half of that amount to go to the Soviet Union.

QUESTION 68: At that time, did the United States have a reparations policy? ANSWER: No. Roosevelt left the lead to Churchill, who opposed such large reparations; but in the end Roosevelt agreed to use the $20 billion figure "as a basis for discussion."

QUESTION 69: Was there contemporary diplomatic opinion that there must have been a link in the Russian mind between their request for exorbitant German reparations and their hope for an American credit? ANSWER: Ambassador Winant "urged at the time that the U.S. consider ways of helping the recovery of the Soviet economy, such assistance to be linked to the achievement of a satisfactory settlement of the problem of German reparations and of the most important political issues between the two Governments."

QUESTION 70: What other opinion is there available on this probable link? ANSWER: Carr has stated: "It seems altogether probable that these two matters, an American credit and German reparations, were closely linked in Soviet political thinking, for our attitude toward both questions profoundly affected the rate of Russia's postwar recovery."

QUESTION 71: Could the Russian loan request have been handled under the heading of Lend-Lease? ANSWER: No, there was strong Congressional sentiment against the use of Lend-Lease for postwar assistance, and a limitation to that effect was actually written into the law in April, 1945. A majority in favor of renewal of the Lend-Lease Act was obtained in the Senate earlier in 1945 only when Vice President Truman broke a tie vote.

QUESTION 72: Why did negotiations for a "Supplementary Agreement" governing credit sales of Lend-Lease equipment to be used for postwar reconstruction fail to bring agreement in the early months of 1945? ANSWER: The Russians insisted on an interest rate of 2 per cent, whereas the U.S. negotiators would not budge from their position that it must be no less than $2^3/8$ per cent.

QUESTION 73: What really lay behind that difference in interest rates? ANSWER: Differing views on tactics. The Russians apparently thought that the fear of postwar unemployment would cause the

United States to yield. The American negotiators were apparently oblivious of the leverage that might be sought in noneconomic matters, and they only feared that the United States would seem overly eager for postwar trade if it acceded to the Russian terms.

QUESTION 74: What finally caused the Russian loan request to be lost in the Washington bureaucracy? ANSWER: The opinion of legal experts that a loan to Russia would contravene a law which ruled out loans to countries that had defaulted on earlier loans—and the Soviet Union had long ago repudiated the debts of the Kerensky government.

QUESTION 75: What was the real reason for the failure of interest to develop in the U.S. government for some settlement that might include the loan sought by the Soviets? ANSWER: The growing disillusionment with Russia over the issue of Poland and the other east European occupied territories. Poland was the major issue between Russia and the West when Truman became President.

QUESTION 76: In the absence of any other means of satisfying the urgent Soviet need for capital assets to further their reconstruction, what was the consequence of Allied disagreements over German reparations? ANSWER: The partition of Germany, brought about— among other reasons—by the Soviet desire to plunder that country.

QUESTION 77: But was not the partition of Germany a cause of the Cold War? ANSWER: Under this analysis, it was not a cause but a consequence. By the time of Potsdam (July 1945), it was clear that the Western powers would not accept the de facto Russian sphere of influence in eastern Europe and that they had nothing to offer Russia to make it forgo the establishment of such a sphere also in central Europe.

QUESTION 78: When was the die then cast and the Cold War begun? ANSWER: In the period between Yalta and Potsdam, when the division of Europe was in effect determined by the relationship of military power as it existed at the time, and when the United States failed to throw into the balance its economic power, which was later to play such an important role in the conduct of the Cold War.

PAUL SEABURY, LOUIS HALLE,
JEAN LALOY, MELVIN CROAN,
E. C. MAY, HUGH SETON-WATSON
Origins of the Post-War Crisis:
A Discussion

THE "ORIGINS OF the Post-war Crisis" were discussed by a panel of historians and political scientists at a special meeting held during the conference organized in London last October by the Institute of Contemporary History (the Wiener Library) in association with the University of Reading. The following is an abridged version of the introductory speeches and of some of the intervenytions that followed. The chair was taken by the Rt. Hon. Kenneth Younger, Director of the Royal Institute of International Affairs.

Paul Seabury: There are two questions about the origins of the Cold War to which I would like to address myself; and first by simply asking, where do we begin if we are to talk about the Cold War? What I think is of crucial importance to the study and examination of an historical epoch, is not the question of who was responsible for something, although this is a legitimate subject of enquiry, and one which has certainly been enquired into by a number of so-called revisionist historians today, but when we are looking back upon this phenomenon known as the Cold War, the large issue, it seems to me, is what *was* the Cold War? That is to say, the quest for a meaning. In fact, a great deal of the confusion about the Cold War as a historical

Mr. Seabury is Professor of Political Science at the University of California at Berkeley.
Mr. Halle is Professor of International Relations at the Institute for Advanced International Studies, Geneva.
Mr. Laloy is a member of the French Foreign Service.
Mr. Croan is Professor of Political Science at the University of Wisconsin.
Mr. May is Professor of History and Dean of the College, Harvard.
Mr. Seton-Watson is Professor of History at the University of London.

From *Journal of Contemporary History* 3 (April, 1968). Reprinted by permission of the Institute for Contemporary History, London, and George Weidenfeld & Nicolson Limited, London.

problem arises from a certain sense of uncertainty as to what it was about; and by what it was about, I mean what the elements of that conflict were.

. . . It has been an East-West conflict, namely a cultural conflict. It has been a conflict over systems of economic organization. It has been a bi-polar struggle between America and the Soviet Union. And also, in a somewhat larger sense, it has been a conflict over what might be called the future of civic polities—in this case the classical terminology used first by Harry Truman, of the Free World against the Totalitarian World. I speak of this as the fusion of these classical elements of the Cold War because it seems to me that its origins, however far back they may be traceable in history, are essentially less important a question than the point in time when all four of these major elements were fused into one large composite thing which we came to call the Cold War. . . . Much of the quarrelling about the origins of the Cold War, and when it happened, seems to me simply to illustrate the uncertainty of many scholars as to what the Cold War was about. . . .

. . . This is one set of propositions I would pose here for discussion. Another kind of problem which seems to me terribly important, when one goes back into the Cold War, is the question of the relationship of conflict to social problems. Many of us, of course, tend to regard conflict in Hobbesian terms, or, even if we are not Hobbesian, we tend to regard conflict as something which is intrinsically bad; and also to regard this intrinsic quality, emerging either from individual or from organized human nature, as one of the worse features of mankind.

One way of looking at this conflict, however, which seems to me particularly important when we look back over the Cold War, is to realize that during the Cold War, as in many other instances in history, conflict was the obverse of something else that was going on. Many historians who deal with the Cold War date its origin from 1945, or 1946, or 1947, and begin with a *tabula rasa* at that point, and then talk about the escalation of the Cold War, or of the downward shift of Soviet-American, Soviet-Western relations, and take it on from there; of course, this is a natural way of delineating things.

If one looks at that point in time when the Cold War began,

wherever it was, one comes to the conclusion that the conditions within which the Cold War began were conditions of almost unmeasurable political chaos; and that in fact—this is an idea which possibly is not terribly original—one can interpret the Cold War as a process of order-building in a situation of extreme chaos and uncertainty. Further, if one looks at the explicit facts, the events of the early part of the Cold War, one notes that at any significant point where this conflict began to develop, it was a point where order was being constructed. In fact, all the rivulets which finally converged into the great flood-river of the Cold War, had their source in the conditions within the European system in 1945, 1946, 1947, when the question of the re-establishment of political order was uppermost in men's minds.

One might even say that the Cold War was a period of time in which order—ironically—was being re-established, rather than to speak of it as a point in time when there was a deterioration and degeneration in the relationships among states. And in fact, what illustrations of this can one find, during that period of five years after the end of the war, where this was not true? In some instances, the specific crises—the Berlin crisis for instance—concerned the founding of a civic polity. What kind of a political system do we want? What kind of a political system is to be created? What kind of economic organization? And in these decisive questions, the Russians and the Americans were there; they had met, and one does not have to be a Greek tragedian to ponder the accidental features of this confrontation, the point again being that in 1945, in many respects, the older organizing principles of the European civic polities had been discredited and shattered, and if that was so, it would in part account for the strength of the organizational ideas which informed the American and Soviet views of this problem and enhanced their strength.

. . . It seems to me that one partial explanation of both Soviet and American behaviour in the uncertain conditions of Europe in the two or three years after the war was the fact that they were asking themselves, what did one do? One was there, one was putting together new systems. What should one do? It is certainly clear on the American side during this time, and especially in the instance of Germany but also in American policies as they developed in respect to eastern Europe, that one pulled out of one's bag one's own devices. . . and it is not a miracle, it seems to me, that the Americans, in these uncertain conditions, turned to their own kind of basic civic principles about how polities should be organized. In Berlin, in eastern Europe, in Italy and elsewhere, where American policy came face to face with this question of what to do when civic polities are destroyed or are apparently unworkable, the temptation was to say, "We will apply here those organizing principles with which we are familiar," and I believe this was as true, on a somewhat smaller scale, of British policy on the European continent, and it certainly was true with respect to the behaviour of the Soviet Union. Things which worked in the Ukraine can as well be applied in Bulgaria, and they were applied by quite similar methods. The point was always the need for action.

So one can regard the Cold War experience, with all its extraordinary tensions, . . . as the years in which the European system was drastically reshaped rather than being destroyed. For this system had been destroyed in the war, and the Cold War, whatever else it meant in the European context, was a point in time where Europe, in the east and in the west, came to re-establish itself along lines quite different from what they had been before.

Finally—a somewhat marginal question—it has seemed to me in the last couple of years that a new school of historiography was beginning to develop, chiefly in the United States, which is not so much concerned with the issues that I am dealing with here, as with the question of responsibility. Whatever the Cold War was, the question is posed: who was responsible for it? When that question is asked, it assumes, of course, that the principal problem is the relationship of America and Russia, Truman and Stalin, American leaders versus Soviet leaders. Who was responsible for the deterioration in those relations? Some of this literature is rather curious, but it seems to me that the question of responsibility for what happened is essentially secondary; that is to say, that when one is dealing with a conflict situation it is much more important first to ascertain what it was that happened, what the intrinsic character of the event was. Then one asks who was responsible. And the second point here is that, since many historians are concerned with this question of responsibility, it is incumbent upon the historian who seeks to write with some degree of authority and definitiveness, in regard to the Cold War above all else, to bear in mind the crucial importance of giving as accurate an account as possible of the sequence of events, so that one does not become constantly the victim of those whose description of events ignores or distorts chronology. This is a characteristic, I believe, of some of the recent examples of revisionist historiography.

Louis Halle: Well, I shall undertake, with the usual over-simplification, to make a few notes in the margin of Mr. Seabury's page, and address myself principally to two questions that he raised in his remarks. One, how early did it begin?—and this is, in a sense, as we all recognize, a semantic question, depending on what you want to call the Cold War; and the related question of who was respon-sible, which is also a question full of pitfalls and trap-doors.

Let me begin by saying that I myself am constantly impressed by the narrow limitations within which leaders of government can exercise this freedom of choice which is supposed to go with their power. There is a paradox here, which I think the general public is not in a good position to appreciate. The President of the United States is the most powerful man in the United States, and perhaps in the world, and he can do anything he pleases, really, and yet, I think every President of the United States has the same impression, that he is the most powerless man in the world and the most frustrated in his efforts to exercise power. I take the example of the President of the United States, but I think it would apply to the Prime Minister of Great Britain, and I am sure that President de Gaulle in privacy sometimes tears his hair at the frustrations of power. Any President of the United States, from the moment he takes office, finds his freedom restricted, in the first place by ten thousand commitments inherited from the past, by ten thousand commitments inherited from history; to use a cliché, he's not writing on a clean slate. . . .

The question that all of us ask, and which is implicit in much of what Mr. Seabury said, is whether the Cold War could not have been averted if Mr. Truman or Mr. Attlee or Mr. Stalin, if any or all of them had taken more intelligent decisions than they did take, if they had not been so stupid, back there in that crucial period of 1945, or should one really say 1944, or 1946, or 1948? But I think it is clear to any historian examining the circumstances, and even clearer to those of us who lived through these events, that these leaders were in large measure the slaves of circumstances; they were the slaves of circumstances that represented the consequences of what had been done in the past. The chief of these circumstances, to my mind, was the power vacuum left at the end of the war in that crucial, vital central area between the western frontier of Russia on one side and the Atlantic Ocean on the other. I do not need to go into what the dynamics of such a situation are. On the record of history, the dynamics of such a situation are quite clear. . . . Any great power that borders on an area that is empty of power—what we call a power vacuum—whatever its disposition, finds it virtually impossible to avoid being drawn further and further into that area, to avoid expansion into that vacuum, until at last it comes up against the retaining wall of some opposing power coming in, let us say, from the other side. And the power in question—let us say hypothetically the Soviet Union—may not want to fill the vacuum itself, but it sees that if it does not, or it believes that if it does not, then a rival power is going to fill it, and this may seem intolerable in terms of its own security. We none of us are able to read Stalin's mind, but I have a fairly strong impression that Stalin in 1945 did not want to expand beyond the relatively narrow strip of countries along Russia's western border that had been under the Tsars before him, and had been traditionally regarded as an essential glacis for the security of Russia. But he did not want—did not intend, perhaps—to go beyond this area, not on account of any morality on his part, or any virtue, but simply because, as a realistic practitioner of power politics, he knew the limits of the area that he could safely control. I am just giving my guess of Stalin's mind, without any authority at all except the record.

But it seems quite clear to me that the dynamics of the situation drew him farther into the power vacuum than he had intended to go. We know, for example, from Djilas's conversations with Stalin, that he did not want a communist take-over in Greece, and that he almost got one anyway, in spite of the fact that he did not want it, because of the dynamics of the situation, and Greece might have been added to his empire against his will. . . .

On the other side, we all know—and here the record, of course, is much more public—that in 1945 the United States was planning to withdraw definitively from Europe in the shortest possible order: "Two years at the outside," said Roosevelt. But the United States then became alarmed by the westward expansion of the Russian Empire and by the prospect that it would continue this expansion to the Atlantic, and so the United States set itself to contain this expanding empire by returning to Europe in 1947–48 and trying to fill what was left of the vacuum so that Russian power should not expand further into it. But what the Americans identified as "containment," looking essentially to their own security, which involved the security of their allies on the other side of the Atlantic, the Russians quite naturally identified as "encirclement," and the ring of encirclement, as it was forged by the United States and its allies, was something that the Russians were almost convulsively impelled to break. And so the great conflict was started. I myself would conclude, then, that the Cold War was made almost inevitable when the wartime leaders took the decision to destroy the German power utterly, to leave a vacuum of power where the German power had formerly been.

However, if one takes this position and examines the decision to create the vacuum of power—the decision made by the wartime leaders at a fairly early stage of the war—one finds that this decision too was made virtually unavoidable by the circumstances of the day, which in their turn represented the consequences of what had been done at a still earlier period. And so one traces the course of history backward, year by year, looking for the point at which it all began. . . .

Looking over this record, I myself feel quite sure that the Cold War could have been averted by a higher quality of statesmanship in the late nineteenth and the early twentieth century. It could have been averted . . . by superb statesmanship at the end of the first world war and in the 1920s, and perhaps . . . it could still have been averted in 1939 and 1940 by statesmanship of such genius as the world has never seen. And after that—after say 1939–40—I think it was simply too late. By 1944 I think we were deluding ourselves dangerously if we believed that a great conflict between Russia and the Atlantic world could still be avoided. We had allowed ourselves over the years to be funnelled into a narrow channel from which there was no longer any escape or any turning back, so that by 1944 the job of statesmanship, it seems to me, was no longer that of avoiding the conflict but rather that of keeping it within such limits as were still feasible; by perhaps such measures as not demobilizing the army of the United States.

But even for this job of keeping the conflict within such limits as were still feasible, the statesmanship of 1944 was incompetent— highly incompetent, totally incompetent; I say this with compassion, not in the way it is usually said, polemically. President Roosevelt had been under pressure beyond human endurance day in and day out for a dozen years. By the end of 1944 he was a dying man, and he really no longer knew what he was doing; he was thoroughly incompetent; he could not read the papers that were put under his eyes; he did not know what it was all about; he was sort of improvising some way or other, and any competent doctor who examined him would have said that he was in no condition to be President of the United States, nor was he in any condition to bear any kind of real responsibility at that time. Mr. Churchill, too, was a sick man who was making decisions the import of which he was no longer able to grasp. We now have Lord Moran's testimony to this effect as well as a series of perfectly clear objective facts on the historical record. As for Stalin, having begun corrupt, he was increasingly corrupted by power and he had for a long time been losing touch increasingly with reality.

In view of all these circumstances, I would myself be unwilling to assign responsibility for the failures that led to the Cold War too glibly, and I can only say that it seems to me a miracle that we are all here in 1967 and still alive.

Jean Laloy: It seems to me that the problem of definition will remain with us when we talk of the Cold War. It is difficult to be precise when referring to such a vague term. What characterizes the Cold War is the idea of unending and irreconcilable rivalry, a battle to which there can be no conclusion. . . . How is it that ever since 1945 one felt, both in Europe and in the United States, that the situation was even worse than it had been before 1939? . . . Three main causes come to mind and are generally accepted by the majority of people who have written on this subject. . . .

The first type, and the one most generally accepted (and the one of which Louis Halle is particularly conscious), is what I will call the traditional cause, that is to say, the problems of power. The vacuum which resulted on the one hand from the break-up of Europe and on the other from the quasi-inevitable confrontation of two armed powers, whatever their intentions with regard to each other. . . .

Still, this kind of explanation is not sufficient when we consider not just the obvious rivalries but the phenomenon of such extreme and total rivalries as the one with which we are faced. . . . The second set of causes could be called imperial. These existed because two major political systems had, for all sorts of reasons, mainly military, extremely conflicting and entangled interests at the end of the war, creating frictions and rivalries which degenerated into hostility which in its turn led to misunderstandings with all their consequences.

I think we will get nearer to an explanation of the problem when we look at the situation from this angle. But even so this does not explain the most surprising characteristic of all; the brutality and totality of the phenomenon in 1945.

This brings us to the third category of explanations to which Schlesinger refers. The word ideological is very unpopular, so I will call them intellectual and moral causes, inherent in the judgment of events reached by the authorities. These include factors covered by the first two categories of causes, but in addition there are also judgments made by individuals which form the basis of decisions, the fact that as a result of this or that judgment this or that decision is taken. In other words, there are those causes originating in the consciousness of those in positions of power, the image they have of themselves, of their aims and the nature of their policies. And this introduces a factor which seems to me of great importance in helping us to understand the differences between the two main powers, the USA and the USSR. The origin of the situation we are discussing is not found only in opposing interests, or in the difference between the military situation of the two sides, but in the fact that they operate by two different codes of conduct and consequently do not understand each other as well as they might. . . .

The Yalta negotiations between Roosevelt and Stalin in February 1945 on the Far East were the traditional type of negotiations concerning spheres of influence, with certain areas reserved to each and certain zones of contact between the two powers in China, with the prospect of eventual co-operation. . . . You there, me here, and between us an area of co-operation. A similar scheme could have been applied to Europe: You want preponderant influence in the East? Okay. We shall retain a certain influence in the West; between us there will be Germany, an area where our interests meet and where we can try to co-operate. Certain elements of stabilization would thus have been created on the basis of a balance of power and interests.

But what happened? What created this phenomenon of extreme disequilibrium, of a sense of oppression in Europe, of anxiety among some of the American leaders, especially General Marshall? What I think happened is that the concept of spheres of influence was quite different on the two sides, and this is an important factor in the situation.

It is quite clear that Stalin had no intention of allowing anyone else any political influence whatsoever in his sphere of influence, in particular in Poland, Rumania, and Bulgaria. (He had similar ideas about Germany, but this is a more complex problem.) His sphere was to be exclusive, and it was because of this conception that the situation became so serious. . . . The Russians, not by deliberate design but because of the nature of the situation, could penetrate the sphere of the other side, whereas the western powers were soon obliged to realize that they had no means of action in east Europe.

The classic spheres of interest which corresponded to the first two types of causes, opposing interests and imperial rivalries, could have been balanced out if they had been comparable; everybody, including the Europeans, had been ready to allot theirs to the Russians. But the result was completely different from the one anticipated; it created inequality between East and West, and this was something for thich the West tried to compensate. . . .

From that moment on reactions on both sides got out of control. If I had to pinpoint the origin of the Cold War, I would do so in the form of a pyramid of causes, starting with the most wide-ranging and the most general, passing through the intermediary area of conflicting interests, and ending up with the final explanation at the level of great political and historical concepts.

There are two further points which I would like to make. First let me come back to Louis Halle's question of whether one could have acted differently. There are probably two or three instances where one might have done so. A bigger economic programme might have been implemented, more attractive for the Soviet Union, in order to give her the feeling that she had a common interest with the United States. That might have been possible. Then there was the big question of Germany, which has never been dealt with properly. During the war no-one dared to deal with the German question as a whole, because each thought that the one who found a satisfactory solution for the German problem would probably also take control of Germany. This was a major difficulty, and the problem should have been investigated more deeply. . . .

The ideas which took shape after the war and which are in fact still with us today might, if they had been applied a little earlier, have produced a somewhat better situation, a slightly better situation at least than that of 1945. People on both sides might have seen things a little more clearly than they did.

If Stalin had hit on a more rational policy in Europe during the war, he might have adopted different methods when it ended. He was fairly cunning, and could be relied on to be cautious. There were alternatives to the policies he chose.

On the western side, I feel that the assessment of Soviet policies in general was wrong. They were too anxious to fit them into a collective framework. In a conversation between Cordell Hull and Molotov in 1943, the American said: "Fortunately you have now come out of your isolationism, so that we will be able to get on with each other." Molotov replied: "Isolationism is a very bad thing!" Hull had illusions, Molotov had none. . . .

Melvin Croan: Let me only suggest that whatever Stalin's aberrations, his abnormal psychology, the Cold War, or something like it, from his point of view made perfectly rational good sense. That is to say the Cold War was, to use the language to which we were treated earlier this week, "system functional" for the Soviet regime. And I must say that my own view of the Soviet Union in world affairs in those initial post-war years is certainly not the one embodied in the official American view of Soviet policy under Stalin, namely that the Soviet Union was hell-bent on expansion, armed to the teeth, ready to begin the march to the Atlantic. Rather I think I tend to subscribe in this case, not to Karl Deutsch's but to Isaac Deutscher's view of the Soviet Union as really a relatively weak pole in the bipolar system: a system, a country, a regime which showed a fearsome face to the outside world but one which was, in the decisive view of its leaders, seriously weakened as a result of the war and potentially vulnerable in the postwar international political system. . . .

I think we must begin by looking at the way in which the post-war Soviet Union must have appeared to its ruler, to Stalin himself. He could not have failed to be aware of Russia's weakness and vulnerability. First of all there was the tremendous loss in population, variously estimated between fifteen and twenty million casualties. Then there was the precipitous decline of industrial production so that, despite the relocation of industry to Siberia, to the Urals, at the end of the war industrial production was only 50 per cent of what it had been in 1939. Moreover, as Stalin must have seen it, one-third of the Soviet post-war population was deemed to have been exposed to what were then called "harmful ideological influences," that is to say, the population of those Soviet territories that had been under German occupation, the population of areas that had been absorbed into the post-war Soviet state and had never been indoctrinated in Marxist-Leninist ideology, the *Ost-Arbeiter,* slave labourers, who had returned from Germany, and, last but not least, those troops who had seen a standard of living in the liberated and occupied areas of Europe to the west of Soviet Russia which was considerably higher than what they had grown up with and considerably at variance with what they had been given to expect. Then we must also consider that, to meet the necessities of survival during the war, the entire apparatus of Soviet government had been considerably transformed in a number of ways. . . .

This is the sense in which it seems to me that ideology was enormously important for the origins of the Cold War. Because if one begins with a sense of a badly-shaken Soviet political system, and if one accepts, as I do, Stalin's consciousness of the need for and utility of absolute dictatorial political power, and if one also adds that Stalin, 66 years old at the end of the war, was bound to consider the struggle for the succession, it seems to me that one gets a series of domestic imperatives which led to the need for an objective enemy. All this was reinforced by Stalin's desire to re-establish the kind of political controls which he deemed necessary for the massive task of reconstruction. In turn, all these objectives, it seems to me, could have been accomplished only through a regeneration of ideology, through—more specifically—the objectification of an external enemy. If one thinks of the alternatives, if one thinks of the conceivable price, from Stalin's point of view, that the Soviet system would have had to pay, or would have run the risk of having to pay, for a continuation of the co-operation, intermittent though it may have been, which occurred during the war between the Soviet Union and the West, then I think one reaches the conclusion that such an alterntive course was quite simply intolerable to Stalin. . . .

These observations leave open the question of whether the Cold War at its most intense and rigid was really inevitable or not. The answer to that question depends on one's philosophy of history, I suppose. All I want to suggest is that a continuation of those tentative lines of co-operation between Russia and the West which had developed during the war was, for a variety of quite understandable domestic Soviet considerations, quite unacceptable to Stalin. Given his point of view, which I regard *not* as the assessment of a madman but rather as the perception of a rather shrewd power-attuned leader, conscious of his own objectives and all too aware of those domestic Soviet realities that seemed to call their attainment into question—something like the Cold War as it actually occurred would have been the likely outcome irrespective of western policies. . . .

Professor E. C. May (Harvard): In a back-handed way, I must come to the defence of the revisionists. It seems to me that in the last three days we have been speaking of the relationship between history and the social sciences and that one of the lines we could possibly pursue is to ask some middle-range theoretical questions with which both social scientists and historians could deal in concrete terms.

One of the obvious ones is how governments arrive at estimates of one another, how they judge the intentions and capabilities of other governments.

This particular case offers such an opportunity as well as any we know, because, speaking in generalities, one can say that the American government, as of the middle of 1944, assumed that co-operation with the Soviet Union was possible, while three years later it viewed the relationship between the two states as inevitably one of hostility. It is, I think, a very interesting question for historians, and for social scientists too, as to how that change in perception and estimation came about. . . .

The revisionist spokesman . . . Mr. Alperovitz, would argue that the change in perception resulted from a change in Presidents. Roosevelt took the view that the United States and the Soviet Union ought to co-operate, Truman came into office and, more limited in vision, thought to use the power of the United States, especially the new power embodied in the atomic bomb, in order to thrust American institutions into Eastern Europe. I do not subscribe to that view. . . .

But there is something to it, for there was certainly a change in perception in America, and I think, following perhaps something Mr. Halle said, that one line an empirical historian might follow is to ask whether or nor there was a change in the American government—a change in the perceiver as well as in what was perceived. I think there are indications that this was in fact so. In the American government, up through 1944, what one would call a foreign affairs bureaucracy was relatively unimportant. The Department of State had had relatively little communication with the President in the pre-war period, when the White House was most interested in domestic affairs. Though things changed, the President himself, for a variety of reasons, did not hold the Foreign Service in very high esteem. He is said to have observed that all he wanted from the Foreign Service was for it to observe neutrality during the war. And when the President became seized of international issues, from 1939 onwards, he relied more and more on military advice in connection with foreign affairs. . . .

In 1944 there began to be increasing realization in sectors of the American bureaucracy that political problems now faced the United States. And one thing that happened, I think, was that, in the first place, there occurred a kind of struggle, though that's too simple a term, between the old Foreign Service group and the new people who had been brought in for post-war planning, out of which the older group emerged triumphant at the end of 1944. Along with some people who came in from the military services, it really dominated the Department of State from that time forward. And perceptions of the world that went to the President—first to Roosevelt and then to President Truman—were the perceptions of different people from those who had been perceiving the world for the President up until the summer of 1944. After that date, the relationship with the Soviet Union was perceived in the Department of State by men who had had a lot of experience in diplomacy in the pre-war period. They knew a good deal more about the Soviet Union than the United Nations planners had known or than the President and his immediate entourage had known. They felt, and with good reason, probably from their experience, very distrustful of the Soviet Union. . . .

Also, along with this, the military services remained advisers to the President and they saw international affairs from their own perspectives, which are perfectly reasonable perspectives. I think Mr. Alperovitz tends to see them as villains for this, but from the standpoint of people, for example, who had built up an Air Force during the war, it was natural to feel alarm that that Air Force might be just dismantled, as seemed likely under the assumptions prevailing earlier. So people in the Air Force, the Navy, and the Army tended to argue the case for a higher level of armament, for maintenance of post-war armaments, and they argued this case in terms of the most realistic possibility—a future clash with the Soviet Union. So from them, too, the President received somewhat different perceptions from those he had been given earlier.

There is one more point I would make. These changes in the bureaucracy coincided with electoral changes inside the United States. The fact that some issues with the Soviet Union related to eastern Europe, coupled with the fact that some leading figures in the Senate came from states that had substantial eastern European constituencies, is not wholly unimportant.

The basic point, however, is that there was a change in the perceiving apparatus and this had some effect on how the government of the United States perceived the Soviet Union. Whether the new perception was more right than the perception that had prevailed before that time seems to me a question that we can really judge only very tentatively. . . .

Professor Hugh Seton-Watson (London): I think we should abolish the phrase "Origins of the Cold War" altogether. I think it is a non-question, a non-subject. It seems to me that there are two real subjects here. One is a long-term condition of basic hostility, between the Soviet Union and the rest of the world, and we can pinpoint the date of that pretty easily, November 1917. . . .

. . . Secondly, it seems to me there is a limited problem of the breakdown of the wartime alliance, and this is what I think we should call it; the breakdown of the wartime alliance is a subject which we can discuss. It is a subject partly of diplomatic history, partly of strategy, partly of internal politics, a huge, vast, interesting, and precise problem. Now, it seems to me that the phrase "Cold War" came into use to describe the hostility. And the point about the hostility was that it was basic whether there was war or peace, and in fact there has never been a war on that particular front; there has never been a war between the Soviet Union and the capitalist world, and one hopes there never will be. But a state of hostility, extremely fundamental, there has always been, and the phrase "Cold War" at the time seemed a very good description of it. . . . The breakdown of the wartime alliance also has causes and these can also be discussed, but they are separate things. We must try to get out of the confusion of mind which has afflicted so many writers on this subject (I suppose to some extent all of us), and which is, I think, due to the following: first of all, when the wartime alliance broke down, there was on the western side, in addition to emotional feelings about the particular subjects we are quarrelling about, an extra, added dimension of bitterness in the form of disillusion about the alliance. There was a very widespread belief that the Russians really are our friends, all that quarrelling about communism is over, we are friends and allies at last, thank God it's ended. And then it hadn't, and the feeling that they had let us down, they are hostile, ungrateful for our aid, welled up, I think, from the grass roots. . . . Secondly, when the alliance was replaced by hostility, and by slanging matches on both sides, tremendous ideological rhetoric poured out from the Soviet side and produced tremendous ideological counter-rhetoric, particularly from the American side. We have phrases (and this one seemed to me nonsense at the time, and certainly has seemed nonsense ever since) like the phrase "Free World," a quite meaningless expression. Or the phrase "liberation," used by the late Foster Dulles—an absurd phrase. And this rhetoric, a sort of escalation of rhetoric on both sides, started, I think, with Soviet rhetoric but there is plenty to make up from the western side. And the third point, of course, is in our own time, the last few years, a very understandable reaction by the younger generation, particularly in the United States, against this rhetoric; they are sick to death of it, particularly when it seems to be justifying this, at first sight inexplicable and grotesque, as it seems to many people, war in Vietnam. So all these things, first the rhetoric and then the indignation against the rhetoric, accusations of the hypocrisy of the fathers' generation and so on, all this has led to a perversion and to complete confusion in our interpretation of the genuine problems of why the alliance broke down, and also the longer term problem of why there was this basic hostility. . . . One last point: if we come back to the question of the breakdown of the alliance, and try to identify precisely its causes, as opposed to the causes of the hostility, it seems to me, in chronological order, they were: first of all Poland, and I really do think that the Polish problem was of the very greatest importance to all the governments concerned; second, what Monsieur Laloy clearly explained to us, this difference in the concept of spheres of influence between Stalin and the West. . . . And thirdly in order of time was, I think, the atomic bomb. I have always thought that the bomb had an anti-Soviet character. The explosion coming when it did, it was designed to some extent to have that character, and the fact that Mr. Alperovitz shows it with great fanfare doesn't seem to me to be a great new discovery. There was an inherently anti-Soviet character in the brandishing of the atomic bomb, and it certainly exacerbated the hostility and produced indignation; but it came in time after the other two, it didn't cause the breakdown, the breakdown had already happened. . . .

CHARLES S. MAIER
Revisionism and the Interpretation
of Cold War Origins

FEW HISTORICAL REAPPRAISALS have achieved such sudden popularity as the current revisionist critique of American foreign policy and the origins of the Cold War. Much of this impact is clearly due to Vietnam. Although the work of revision began before the United States became deeply involved in that country, the war has eroded so many national self-conceptions that many assumptions behind traditional Cold War history have been cast into doubt. For twenty years the Soviet-American conflict was attributed to Stalin's effort to expand Soviet control through revolutionary subversion, or, as in a more recent formulation, to "the logic of his position as the ruler of a totalitarian society and as the supreme head of a movement that seeks security through constant expansion." Revisionist assailants of this view have now found readers receptive to the contrary idea that the United States must bear the blame for the Cold War. The preoccupation with America's historical guilt distinguishes the new authors not only from anti-communist historians but from earlier writers who felt the question of blame was inappropriate. William McNeill, for example, in an outstanding account written at the height of the Cold War, stressed a nearly inevitable falling-out among allies who had never been united save to fight a common enemy. This viewpoint has been preserved in some recent accounts; but since Denna Fleming's massive Cold War history of 1961, the revisionists have gone on to indict the United States for long-term antipathy to communism, insensitivity to legitimate Soviet security needs, and generally belligerent behavior after World War II.

The revisionist version of Cold War history includes three major elements: an interpretation of Eastern European developments; an

Mr. Maier is Assistant Professor of History at Harvard.

Excerpted without footnotes and bibliography from Charles Maier, "Revisionism and the Interpretation of Cold War Origins" in *Perspectives in American History*, IV, 1970. By permission of Charles S. Maier.

allegation of anti-Soviet motives in the Americans' use of the atomic bomb; and a general Marxian critique of the alleged American search for a world capitalist hegemony. Since these three elements comprise a detailed reassessment of the role of the United States in world politics they deserve to be discussed and evaluated in turn; but in the end one must consider the more fundamental question of the conceptual bases of revisionist history.

The revisionists are divided among themselves about the turning points and the causes of American aggressiveness, but all agree that the traditional description of the crucial events in Eastern Europe must be radically altered. The old version of the roots of the Cold War charged Soviet Russia with progressively tightening totalitarian control from mid-1944. In effect the earlier historians only confirmed the diagnosis of Ambassador Averell Harriman in Moscow, whose cables between 1943 and early 1945 changed from emphasizing the needs of a functioning wartime alliance to stressing the difficulties of prolonging cooperation in the face of Soviet ambitions. . . . It was agreed after 1945 that the germs of the Cold War lay in Stalin's intransigence on the Polish issue.

In contrast to this interpretation, the revisionists charge that the United States forced Stalin into his stubborn Polish policy by backing the excessive aspirations of the exile Polish government in London. Revisionist accounts emphasize how antagonistic the State Department's refusal to sanction any territorial changes during the war must have appeared in Moscow. . . . At the Yalta conference, Stalin agreed to add some Western Poles to the communist-based government and to move toward free elections; and if the United States had continued to accept the Yalta provisions in a generous spirit, the revisionists maintain, the earlier disputes might have been overcome. . . .

This American attitude toward Polish issues, the revisionists claim, was typical of a wide range of Eastern European questions where the United States appeared to be set upon frustrating Russia's international security. From the summer of 1945 Truman and Byrnes, it is charged, sought to reverse the pro-Soviet governments in Rumania and Bulgaria by blustering with atomic weapons. The American opposition to Soviet demands for territorial security and friendly neighboring states allegedly forced the Russians away from their minimal aims of 1943–1945, which envisaged United Front coalition regimes, to the ruthless communization they imposed by 1947–1948. Had the United States not demanded total openness to Western influence, the revisionists imply, Poland, Bulgaria, and Rumania might have survived as Hungary and Czechoslovakia did until 1947–1948 and Finland thereafter. But in fact, they argue, the parties and social groups that Washington desired to entrench could only intensify Stalin's mistrust. In revisionist eyes these groups were either unworthy or unviable: unworthy because they regrouped pre-war reactionary elements who had often been pro-German, unviable because even when democratic they were doomed to fall between the more intransigent right and the Russian-backed left.

Even more fundamental from the revisionist point of view, there was no legitimacy for any American concern with affairs in that distant region. However ugly the results in Eastern Europe, they should not really have worried Washington. Russia should have been willingly accorded unchallenged primacy because of her massive wartime sacrifices, her need for territorial security, and the long history of the area's reactionary politics and bitter anti-bolshevism. Only when Moscow's deserved primacy was contested did Stalin embark upon a search for exclusive control. These revisionist assessments of the United States's political choices in Eastern Europe are valid in some respects, simplistic in others. . . .

. . . Despite revisionist implications to the contrary, the major offense of the middle- and pro-Western groups in Soviet eyes was not really their collusion with rightists. The Russians themselves, after all, supported the far more fascist-tainted Marshall Badoglio as Italian premier. The major crime of the pro-Western elements seems really to have been the desire to stay independent of Soviet influence in a situation of Soviet-American polarization that made independence seem enmity. Perhaps the pro-Westerners acted imprudently by looking to Washington: Benes won three years of Czech democracy by collaboration with Moscow—but one might argue from his example that either the collaboration prolonged the Czech respite or that it helped contribute to the final undermining of Prague's independence. In any case the outcome throughout the area was communist dictatorship. Between 1945 and 1947 the peasant party and social democratic leaders were harassed in their assemblies and organizations, tried for treason by communist interior ministries, driven abroad or into silence, and finally, as with the case of Nikola Petkov, the Bulgarian agrarian party leader, executed.

This bleak result naturally undercut those who advocated voluntarily relinquishing United States influence in the area. Opposing the official American rejection of spheres of influence, Henry Wallace on one side, and Henry Stimson and George Kennan on the other, counseled restraint and acceptance of the new status quo; but few contemporary advocates could wholeheartedly celebrate a policy of spheres of influence. It was justified from expedience and as a second-best alternative. As a former advocate recalls, it had always to be advanced as a melancholy necessity, especially as the men for whom Western liberals felt most sympathy were liquidated. To follow a policy of abnegation might indeed have allowed more openness in Eastern Europe; on the other hand, the Stalinist tendencies toward repression might well have followed their own Moscow-determined momentum.

If as a group the revisionists condemn the American role in Eastern Europe, they diverge beyond that point of criticism. One major area of debate among them concerns the use of the atomic bomb, which while it must be weighed as an important issue in its own right also signals a basic methodological division. Although the revisionist writing that often seems most hostile to received opinion is that of Gar Alperovitz he is not the most radical of the dissenting historians. His writings involve a less thoroughgoing critique of United States institutions than the contributions of either William Appleman Williams or Gabriel Kolko. What has elevated Alperovitz to the role of the revisionist *enfant terrible* is his thesis that the United States used nuclear weapons against the Japanese largely to overawe the Soviets. Still, his version of events hinges less on structural elements in American life than on the contingent roles of personality and technological opportunity.

There are two aspects of Alperovitz's thesis: first, that before Hiroshima, expectation of the bomb's availability caused decisive tactical changes in American diplomacy; second, that the weapon was used wantonly when it became available, in part to limit Soviet penetration into the Far East, and more generally because only a combat demonstration would create a sufficient impression to prevent absolute Soviet control over Eastern Europe. Only the desire to have the atomic bomb in hand, Alperovitz argues, led Truman to reverse his harsh diplomatic approach of late April 1945, to dispatch Harry Hopkins to Moscow, and to delay the Potsdam conference despite Churchill's misgivings.

More disturbing than this charge is Alperovitz's subsequent argument that Americans did not merely wish to possess the bomb but actually used it to enhance the country's position vis-à-vis the Soviets. . . . But whether calculations about the bomb were decisive remains unproven. The evidence adduced must remain circumstantial: the increased hostility to Russia that was thrust upon the new President; Stimson's and Brynes' awareness that possession of nuclear weapons might bestow significant diplomatic leverage; and the pushing back of a Big Three parley. In light of this conjunction of events a calculated strategy of delay, such as Alperovitz develops, does remain a possible component of Truman's motivation. But the initial months of the new administration formed a period of contradictory needs and approaches. For a while Truman may have been thinking in terms of disengaging from the disquieting Soviet repression in Bulgaria and Rumania by withdrawing from the Allied Control Commission rather than attempting to reverse the course of events by exerting pressure within it. The Hopkins mission was well suited to many purposes: perhaps an effort to appease Stalin until nuclear weapons were at hand, but more immediately an attempt to secure agreements in their own right and to halt further deterioration of relations as a worthy goal in itself. For Truman, as even Alperovitz realizes, the Hopkins trip was probably viewed not as a reversal of his earlier harsh language to Molotov on April 23, but as a complementary démarche, another approach to a dramatic unjamming of issues.

What also makes the Alperovitz view so difficult to evaluate is the fact, as the author himself admits, that the debate has been largely a retrospective one. Actors at the time hardly saw the significance of the alternatives as later historians have. The place that the idea of using the bomb might have been thrashed out was in the so-called Interim Committee dominated by Stimson and Byrnes, both of whom were committed to dropping the weapon. In this forum it was easy to dismiss any alternative to the incineration of a real city as beset with one fatal obstacle or another. And beyond the Interim Committee except for a group of scientific dissenters at Chicago who felt they had been turned into sorcerers' apprentices, there was no fundamental challenge to using the weapon. Moreover, if the bomb represented a threshhold in terms of weapons technology, it no longer represented one in terms of casualties: the Tokyo incendiary raids in March of 1945 produced about 84,000 deaths; Dresden, between 60,000 and 130,000; Hiroshima, about 70,000. The significant ethical question was that of area versus precision bombing, and the allies had long since steeled their conscience on that issue. If the Navy and Air Force, moreover, were confident that they could starve the Japanese into submission, the Joint Chiefs never gave their collective imprimatur to such a view because the Army would not endorse it. Many thought the collapse of Japan was likely; official plans were drawn up to deal with a sudden surrender; but no one in authority felt he could assume official responsibility for advocating restraint so long as some prolonged Japanese resistance was remotely possible. If Byrnes, Harriman, and Admiral Leahy would have preferred to complete the Pacific war without obligations to Moscow, Truman still felt it his duty to cling to the contingency plans of the Joint Chiefs of Staff and seek Soviet help at Potsdam. Even at Potsdam when Japanese capitulation seemed near, a host of factors militated against reappraisal: the ambivalence of the Tokyo response to the Potsdam ultimatum (itself only the vaguest of warnings); concern that die-hard Japanese militarists would seek to "protect" their monarch against those who counseled surrender; the debate in Washington over retention of the Emperor, which delayed a surrender formula both sides might accept; the belief that the nation responsible for the Pearl Harbor attack could be requited from the air hundreds of times over without any injustice; and no doubt the vested interests in making the bomb contribute to the war effort. If in addition to these pressures Byrnes also entertained an ulterior anti-Soviet motive, it probably represented a marginal, additional payoff of a policy long established on other grounds.

Alperovitz seems to feel it wrong that the atomic bomb became a major factor in American policy calculations. Certainly, however, it was natural to give deep consideration to the new weapon's diplomatic implications. And despite Alperovitz's linkage, there is insufficient evidence that possession of nuclear weapons was decisive in motivating a hard line on Bulgaria and Rumania in the latter half of 1945. This approach followed naturally from the administration's view of Eastern European developments since Yalta and would have been pursued without an atomic monopoly. It is questionable, too, whether the United States could have utilized a veiled atomic threat except in regard to the distant future, for Washington was not prepared to threaten the use of nuclear weapons over Russian targets in 1945. Despite the revisionist view that the United States enjoyed a preponderance of power and therefore must be charged with the greater responsibility in the generation of the Cold War, the Soviet Union still exerted effective control over the area that was central to the dispute. This is not to deny that outside its borders the United States seemed to be flaunting its nuclear capacity. Harriman reported from Moscow in November that the Soviets felt America was trying to intimidate them with the atomic bomb, while to observers in Washington Truman and Byrnes often seemed bolstered by an inner assurance of American invincibility.

Indeed it may have appeared by late 1945 and early 1946 as if the United States were wrapping iron fist in iron glove; but even had there been a far more sophisticated and reserved approach, the simple fact of one-sided possession of the bomb was bound to evoke mistrust. There was no way for its influence to be exorcized from international relations.

Alperovitz's charges are, of course, profoundly disquieting. But at least he suggests that things might have been different. Had Roosevelt lived he might have smoothed out differencs with Moscow. Had Stimson been heeded, the United States might have bargained by offering to share atomic secrets and not by seeking, as it is alleged to have done, to intimidate with the weapon itself. Gabriel Kolko, in contrast, can dismiss Alperovitz's arguments about atomic diplomacy because they are unnecessary for what he considers the more important indictment, namely, that the United States, in order to serve its economic needs and ambitions, opposed any threat to its world-wide military and political power.

This view produces a more radical interpretation of both American foreign relations and the country's internal history. William Appleman Williams, for instance, argues that the long-term American quest for universal market and investment arenas, even into Eastern Europe, naturally collided with quite moderate Soviet wartime aspirations and thereby helped the Kremlin's own hard-liners and ideologues to prevail. For both Williams and Kolko, moreover, a critique of United States foreign policy forms only part of a wider reassessment of American liberal institutions. The anti-communist effort is depicted as the natural product of an industrial society in which even major reform efforts have been intended only to rationalize corporate capitalism.

The more the revisionists stress the continuity of American capitalist goals and de-emphasize the importance of the Roosevelt-Truman transition, the more they tend to condemn all of America's earlier policies as contributing to the Cold War. The revisionists in general have stressed the direct pre-1945 clashes with the Soviets. . . . All revisionists are mindful of the Western treatment of the Soviets as a pariah regime.

The more radical revisionists, however, go on to depict all of twentieth-century foreign policy as woven into a large counter-revolutionary fabric of which the Cold War itself is only one portion. . . . Even before Wilson the roots of the Cold War can be discerned, they feel, in the economic lobbying that backed the Open Door policy and the capitalist expansion of the late nineteenth century. Finally, under the stresses of a market economy, even the otherwise virtuous farmers felt it necessary to seek world markets and back imperialist expansionism. The private economy, for Williams and others, taints with acquisitiveness the Jeffersonian Eden that America might have been.

There is a further aspect of this radical revisionism. Since it concentrates on American expansionism in general, its focus shifts from the Soviet-American conflict to the alleged American imperialist drive against all forces of radicalism, or what Kolko loosely calls the New Order. Not an insouciant blundering, and not the arrogance of power, but only capitalist megalomania suffices to explain American efforts to prop up an international Old Order of discredited and outworn parties and elites. Within this perspective, Kolko's explanation of the events of 1943–1945 becomes most clear. He offers three major areas of evidence: United States policy in respect to its future enemy, that is, the effort to reduce Russia to dependency; United States policy against its own ally, that is, the insistence on an economic multilateralism designed to reduce Great Britain to dependency; and United States policy in respect to the "Third World" and the Resistance, the effort to smash all truly independent challenges to American hegemony.

Under Kolko's scrutiny the policies once adjudged to be among the most enlightened emerge as the most imperialistic. . . . In the final analysis American efforts amounted to a subtle neo-colonialism. While classical economic theorists helped to justify the international division of labor by comparative-advantage doctrine no matter how unequal the partners, the revisionists evidently feel that the costs to the less powerful or industrial nation outweigh the benefits. They emphasize that specialization can act to perpetuate relations of dependency, and they view American policy as dedicated throughout the twentieth century to fostering the bonds of economic subordination. In this interpretative framework the Cold War, in its European aspects, arose because Soviet Russia refused to allow herself or Eastern Europe to be integrated into the American neo-colonial network.

This analysis is often illuminating but sometimes exaggerated and tendentious. . . . The revisionists' reasoning . . . fits in analytically with one of their major current preoccupations: the role of the United States in the third world of peasant movements. The same revisionist argument that sees foreign trade as a means to subordination and control also suggests that the United States had to be hostile to movements seeking genuine self-determination and local independence. . . .

This concern with the continuities of counter-revolution arises in part from the natural fact that revisionists want to explain the origins of cold war against the background of Vietnam. Ironically enough, the result is to downgrade the importance of the Soviet-American antagonism that originally preoccupied revisionist authors. What in fact increasingly distinguishes the more radical historians is their emphasis upon a Soviet "conservatism" that sought to discourage revolutionary action for the sake of acquiring territorial buffers. Stalin's treaty with Chiang at the expense of Mao, his distrust of Tito, and his abandonment of the Greek Communists, complement American objectives. In view of this supposed convergence of Moscow and Washington, the Cold War becomes little more than a mistaken enmity deriving from the United States' panicky identification of Soviet policies with indigenous Marxist or merely democratic movements. This finding confirms a "third world" viewpoint which can indict both major world powers and supply a "usable past" for those morally overwhelmed by an updated Holy Alliance between Moscow and Washington. Through the mid 1960's, in short, the revisionists could still be fixed upon explaining the origins of conflict with Moscow; by the end of the decade they were concerned with the antagonism with Havana, Hanoi, and Peking.

Attractive though it may be in light of current events, this third-world perspective has serious analytical deficiencies. First of all, its Marxian basis imposes an overly schematic view of motivation; it precludes any possibility that American policy-makers might have acted from genuine emancipatory impulses or even in uncertainty. . . . What is perhaps most misleading about the neo-Marxian point of view is its suggestion that Europe in 1945 was as socially malleable as underdeveloped societies today. By projecting a third-world image upon the West the revisionists overestimate the power of the radical forces and the structural possibilities for change. The United States did help to brake fundamental change especially after V-E Day, but the major limits on reconstruction were set by the internal divisions within the Resistance and the conservative attitude of the Communist parties and the other two allies.

No more in institutional than in political terms did America alone abort a New Order. Kolko's New Order represents a normative image of revolution borrowed from predominately peasant countries or Yugoslavia and applied to industrial Europe. But not even 1945 Europe was so shaky. . . . A renovation of society on new principles would have required smashing the corporate pluralism in which left-wing as well as conservative leaders found comfort. America did not really have to rescue Europe from radical change because no significant mass-based elements advocated a radical transformation.

The so-called New Order—an amalgam in the revisionist mind of Yugoslavian factory councils and Algerian, Vietnamese, or Greek national resistance movements—had no solid peacetime constituency in the West.

What in fact was new in the West was precisely the conglomeration of business, labor, and government that the revisionists lament. In America the New Deal and the wartime economic effort worked to dissolve many of the old lines between public and private spheres. In Fascist Italy, Vichy France, and Nazi Germany a similar interweaving occurred, as it did in a democratic Britain that submitted to extensive planning and welfare measures. Revisionists such as Kolko would accept this description of trends—in fact, Kolko examined the precursor of this private-public interpenetration in his critique of Progressivism—but the revisionists regard these developments as clearly elitist and conservative. Ultimately their general interpretation conceives of the issues behind the Cold War in terms of inequality and class: the Cold War represents to them a continuation of an international civil war in which Russian and later peasant revolutionary forces have successively championed the cause of the oppressed in all countries, while the United States has become the leader of the world's elites.

But no matter what importance this conceptualization may have for today's world, it obscures the historical development. If there has been a growth in international class conflict over the past generation, so too in Western societies there has been an increase of bureaucratic and administrative solutions for social conflict—solutions to which labor contributed, solutions that were conservative in leaving intact private control and ownership, yet still social compromises that commanded wide assent. The forces for compromise sprang from the bureaucratic trends of modern industrial society as they existed in Europe as well as in the United States. The revisionist view splits the world into an industrial half that America supposedly stabilized on behalf of a bureaucratic capitalism and a peasant world where the United States has since met its match. But if peasant society has proved hard to manipulate, Western industrial society has also proved refractory; the neo-Marxians overestimate the fragility of its capitalist order, and overvalue the American contribution to counter-revolution as well as the will to impose it.

There is still no well-modulated portrayal of what the United States sought in the world, even less of the real possibilities of institutional change.

No full evaluation of revisionist history, however, can be content with weighing particular interpretations against available evidence. For beneath the details of specific revisionist arguments are more fundamental historiographical problems—implicit conceptual models and underlying assumptions about the decisive factors in American foreign relations.

The revisionists' approach to international conflict and foreign policy formation is a narrow one. They are interested in certain specific modes of explanation and no others. Rejecting any model of international society that sees crucial impulses to conflict as inherent in the international system itself, they seek explanations in American domestic conditions. But for them all domestic conditions are not equally valid. They are unwilling to accept any description that tends to stress the decentralized nature of decision-making or that envisages the possibility of expansionist policy taking shape by imperceptible commitments and bureaucratic momentum. Above all, they approach history with a value system and a vocabulary that appear to make meaningful historical dialogue with those who do not share their framework impossible.

The revisionists presuppose international harmony as a normal state and have a deep sense of grievance against whatever factors disturb it. This common assumption shapes their work from the outset in terms of both analysis and tone. But is international harmony a normal state? The division of sovereignty among nation-states makes it difficult to eliminate friction and tension, as theorists from the time of Machiavelli and Hobbes have pointed out. The disputes of 1944–1945 especially were not easy to avoid. With a power vacuum in Central Europe created by the defeat of Germany and with the expansion of American and Soviet influence into new, overlapping regions, some underlying level of dispute was likely. Angered by the scope that the Cold War finally assumed, the revisionists do not really ask whether conflict might have been totally avoided or what level of residual disagreement was likely to emerge even with the best intentions on both sides.

Once mutual mistrust was unchained—and much already existed—all disputes were burdened by it. The initiatives that would have been required to assuage incipient conflict appeared too risky to venture in terms either of domestic public opinion or international security. By late 1945 the United States and Russia each felt itself to be at a competitive disadvantage in key disputes. Each felt that the other, being ahead, could best afford to make initial concessions, while gestures on its part would entail disproportionate or unilateral sacrifice. Perhaps more far-sighted leaders could have sought different outcomes, but there were pressures on all policy-makers to take decisions that would harden conflict rather than alleviate it. Some details on this point are particularly worth considering.

In retrospect there appear to have been several areas of negotiation where compromise might at least have been possible, where accommodation demanded relatively little cost, and where the continued absence of greater concession probably deepened suspicion. Some additional flexibility on the issues of both atomic control and financial assistance might have helped to alleviate the growing estrangement. Innovative and generous as our plans for atomic energy control appeared to Americans at the time, the provisions for holding all United States weapons until controls were complete, as well as the demand that the Russians renounce their United Nations veto on all atomic-energy matters, probably doomed the proposal. With such an imbalance of obligations the Soviet advocates of their own country's atomic arsenal were likely to prevail over those willing to acquiesce in nuclear inferiority for a decade or so. As so often after 1946, the reluctance to give up an advantage that at best could only be transitory led to a further spiral in the arms race.

With far less objective risk than was presented by the nuclear issue, liberality with aid might also have offered United States policy-makers a chance to dissipate quarrels. Unfortunately Lend-Lease was brusquely cut off in a way that could not help but offend the Russians, although it was slated to end with the close of the war in any case. Had transitional aid or a significant post-war loan been available, the termination of Lend-Lease might not have proved so abrasive. But the loan proposal was always keyed to the extraction of political concessions, and the Russians had no need to become a suppliant. As it turned out a post-was credit was less crucial to the Soviets than to the British who faced a mammoth balance of payments crisis that Russia did not have to cope with. Washington could not really use the loan to wrest concessions, instead her failure to provide funds precluded any chance for post-war credits to help improve the general international atmosphere and re-establish some minimal trust.

Disagreement at the start over Eastern Europe had undermined the chances of those peripheral initiatives that might in turn have helped to alleviate overall tension. By becoming trapped in a position where apparently unilateral démarches were needed to break a growing deadlock, policy was far more likely to be vetoed by State Department, Congress, or the President's immediate advisers. It was far harder to justify financial assistance or atomic renunciation when Russia was already felt to be uncooperative. Domestic constraints and the suspicions fed by international rivalry interacted to intensify a serious deadlock.

Although the revisionists do not readily soften their judgments about American policy-makers in light of these pressures, they do use them to make Soviet responses appear more acceptable. They explain that the Russians had to reckon with the death of an exceptionally friendly President and the replacement of his key policy-makers by tougher spokesmen; with a tooth-and-nail resistance to the German reparations that Russia felt she clearly deserved; and with the curt United States dismissal of a Soviet voice in the occupation of Japan, an influence over the Dardanelles, and a base in the Mediterranean. Neither side was likely to see in the opposing moves anything but a calculated effort to expand power, or, with a little more subtlety, the upshot of a contest between the other power's doves and hawks with the doves increasingly impotent. Such interpretations tended to produce a response in kind. In the absence of any overriding commitment to conciliation, the Cold War thus contained its own momentum toward polarization and deadlock.

It would, however, also be inappropriate to fix too much blame for the origins of the Cold War upon the Hobbesian nature of the international system, though it is a major element the revisionists ignore. As revisionists insist, domestic factors are clearly required to explain the timing and trajectory of the Soviet-American antagonism. But significantly absent from revisionist writing is any sense of the bureaucratic determinants of policy—an element of increasing interest to historians and social scientists seeking to respond to the revisionist indictment. In the view of these writers, decisions are seen as the outcome of organizational disputes within an overall government structure. Policy emerges not so much as a way of maximizing a well-defined national "interest" as the outcome of struggles among bureaucratic forces each seeking to perpetuate its own *raison d'être* and to expand its corporate influence. Recent studies have shown for instance that much of the impulse toward a cold-war defense posture after 1945 came from the fact that both the Air Force and the Navy sought out new strategic conceptions and justifications to preserve their wartime size and status.

Study of the German and reparations issues also reveal how American foreign policy emerged from inter-departmental contention, in this case between Henry Morgenthau and the Treasury on the one hand, and on the other a more conservative State Department desirous of recreating economic stability in Central Europe. After V-E day the Army military government agencies also demanded that their American occupation zone be as economically self-sufficient as possible. The result of these pressures, and of Morgenthau's loss of influence under Truman, was that the United States quarreled bitterly with the Soviets to limit reparations. The American insistence at Potsdam that each power largely confine its reparations to its own zone helped lead to the very division of Germany that the United States officially deplored. The intent was not to build Germany up at the expense of Russia: Byrnes after all offered the Soviets a 25 or 40-year treaty against German aggression in late 1945 and the spring of 1946. But each agency's struggle for the priorities it set in terms of its own organizational interest helped shape a narrow policy that was not subordinated to a clear sense of our more general relations with the Soviet Union.

This approach to policy analysis, which opens up a new range of motivation and offers an alternative to an undue emphasis on personal factors, contrasts with the explanatory model suggested by the neo-Marxist revisionists. For the latter group what ultimately explains policy is a "system" arising out of the property and power relations within a society, a system causative in its own right and within which institutions and organizations do not lead independent lives but relate to each other dialectically. For these revisionists the explanation of events in terms of intra-governmental structure and struggles is simply formalistic, oriented to the procedural aspects of policy formation and begging the substantive questions. For them, the processes of government might as well be a black box: if one understands the distribution of wealth and influence then policy follows by an almost deductive logic. To attribute decisive influence to bureaucratic pressures seems additionally frivolous to the revisionists since allegedly only certain elites ever rise to the top of those bureaucracies. For those, on the other hand, who stress the political infighting among bureaucracies what is important about history tends to be the successive modifications of action—in short, political process not social structure.

Both of these approaches are deceptive and limiting if taken to extremes. For those who stress history as bureaucratic process, all questions of historical responsibility can appear ambiguous and even irrelevant. Foreign policy emerges as the result of a competition for fiefs within governmental empires. Bureaucratic emphases can produce a neo-Rankean acquiescence in the use of power that is no less deterministic than the revisionist tendency to make all policies exploitative in a liberal capitalist order. But what is perhaps most significant about these alternative causal models is that they are addressed to different questions. The non-revisionists are asking how policies are formed and assume that this also covers the question why. The revisionists see the two questions as different and are interested in the why. And by "why?" revisionists are asking what the meaning of policies is in terms of values imposed from outside the historical narrative. The revisionists charge that the historian must pose this question of meaning consciously or he will pose it unconsciously and accept the values that help to uphold a given social system. History, they suggest, must serve the oppressors or the oppressed, if not by intent then by default. The historian who wishes to avoid this iron polarity can reply that social systems rarely divide their members into clear-cut oppressors and oppressed. He can also insist that even when one despairs of absolute objectivity there are criteria for minimizing subjectivity. On the other hand, he must also take care that the history of policy making not become so focused on organizational processes that the idea of social choice and responsibility is precluded.

In the end it is this attempt by the revisionists to analyze specific historical issues on the basis of *a priori* values about the political system that most strongly affects the controversies their writings have touched off. For their values cannot be derived from the mere amassment of historical data nor do they follow from strictly historical judgments, but rather underlie such judgments. This is true in some sense, no doubt, of history in general, but the whole of Cold War historiography seems particularly dependent upon defined value systems.

For the revisionists, on the one hand, the key issues hinge not upon facts or evidence but upon assessments as to how repressive or non-repressive contemporary liberal institutions are. These judgments in turn must be made within ground rules that allow only polar alternatives for evaluating political action. What is nonrevolutionary must be condemned as counter-revolutionary, and reformist political aspirations are dismissed in advance. Similarly, the foreign policies of Western powers cannot escape the stigma of imperialism, for imperialism and exploitation are defined by the revisionists as virtually inherent in any economic intercourse between industrialized and less developed states, or just between unequals. But how can one decide whether the economic reconstruction that America financed was beneficial or "exploitative" for countries brought into a cooperative if not subordinate relationship to the United States? How does one judge the value of multilateral or bilateral trading relations that benefit each side differentially? Judgments must rest upon definitions of exploitation or fairness that logically precede the historical narrative and cannot be derived from it.

The non-revisionist, on the other hand, can refuse to accept the ground rules that presuppose exploitation, dependency, or automatic neo-colonialism; he can refuse to accept the definitions that allow no choice between revolution and reaction. But traditional Cold War historians no less than the revisionists have been involved in tautologies. Historical explanations are normally tested by efforts to find and weigh contradictory evidence, but Cold War analyses on both sides have relied upon propositions that cannot be disproven. Sometimes disproof is precluded by prior assumptions, and while revisionists may believe America's capitalist economy necessitates a voracious expansionism, Cold War theorists have similarly argued that any commitment to communism is *ipso facto* destructive of a "moderate" or "legitimate" international order. Often disproof is impossible because the explanations are totalistic enough to accommodate all contradictory phenomena into one all-embracing explanatory structure. So writers who condemned the Soviets cited Marxist ideology as evidence of real intention when it preached revolution and as evidence of deviousness when it envisaged United-Front coalitions. Conversely, according to the revisionists, when the United States withdrew foreign assistance it was seeking to bring nations to heel; when it was generous, it sought to suborn. When the United States bowed to British desires to delay the Second Front it justified Soviet suspicions; when it opposed Churchill's imperial designs it did so in order to erect a new economic hegemony over what England (and likewise France or the Netherlands) controlled by direct dominion. Spokesmen for each side present the reader with a total explanatory system that accounts for all phenomena, eliminates the possibility of disproof, and thus transcends the usual processes of historical reasoning. More than in most historical controversies, the questions about what happened are transformed into concealed debate about the nature of freedom and duress, exploitation and hegemony. As a result much Cold War historiography has become a confrontation *manqué*—debatable philosophy taught by dismaying example.

WALTER LAFEBER

War: Cold

CARL BECKER ONCE observed that a professor is a man who thinks otherwise. One might add that a professor is often a person who professes and that a history professor is one who professes history, at least most of the time.

These are essential traits of a group which is becoming known for advocating a new revision of post-1945 American diplomatic history. The new revisionists think otherwise because they have not accepted the American government's explanation of how and why the Cold War developed.

They have, moreover, revised and challenged the work of those most influential historians, who might best be identified as the Liberals, who have essentially followed the government's explanations in writing their own histories of the Cold War. Often identified also as "New Left," these revisionists have such widely-varying relationships to that term that they are perhaps better studied through their view of history rather than their call to politics. . . .

After World War II, revisionists have believed that the fundamental error was a gross miscalculation of Communism and Russian Communist intentions. They argue that in the 1944-1946 years, Stalin had considerably more flexibility and posed a less aggressive threat to the West than the Liberals have been willing to admit.

The revisionists of course will have nothing to do with those who argue that Communism as an ideological monolith continues to be the enemy, that Chinese or North Vietnamese Communism has picked up where Stalinism and North Korean Communism left off. But between these two groups (the revisionists on the one hand and the current Vietnam Cold Warriors on the other), there is a middle group with which the revisionists disagree also.

Mr. LaFeber is Professor of History at Cornell.

From "War: Cold" by Walter LaFeber, *Cornell Alumni News,* October, 1968. Reprinted by permission of *Cornell Alumni News,* Walter LaFeber, and John Wiley and Sons, Inc.

COMMUNISM: MONOLITHIC OR NOT?

These historians in the middle have argued that Communism as an ideology cannot be dismissed as a threat to American interests, and this group has often focused particularly upon the threat posed by the far left within American society. Flourishing in the late 1940s with Reinhold Niebuhr as its intellectual godfather and Arthur Schlesinger Jr.'s *The Vital Center* as its call to action, the emphasis upon the role of Communist ideology, particularly as that ideology acted as a primary cause of the split between East and West in 1945, recently reappeared in Mr. Schlesinger's influential article on the causes of the Cold War in the October 1967 issue of *Foreign Affairs*. . . .

In analyzing American motivations, revisionists have made American expansionism a central issue in the Cold War debate. Oglesby has phrased it most bluntly: "America's expansionism is not debatable. It is a dynamic condition which describes our national career better than any other single term. It is not concealed; it is celebrated. All those sermons on the need to spread the American Way of Life are not just jokes—they are real sermons, and they come from a culture which really thinks its survival requires more and more converts."

No historian challenges this stress upon expansion. The differences occur when the questions arise of what were the motivations and results of the expansion, and can and should the expansion continue.

Revisionists are quite clear about the general motivations. Again to quote Oglesby: "Recall that the foreign policies of the nation-states are essentially continuations of their domestic policies." One of the many consequences of which flow from that assumption is the revisionist argument that the dramatic confrontation after World War II resulted primarily from the American attempt to wield pre-eminent power because domestic economic, political, and social interests demanded the movement of that power into far-flung areas of the world, particularly Central and Eastern Europe. (Within this broad consensus revisionists disagree. Williams and Oglesby, for example, express considerably more fundamental criticisms of the American system than does Fleming.)

The Liberals, on the other hand, argue in terms of outside influences: a vacuum in Central and Western Europe and the threatened movement of Soviet power into that vacuum forced the United States to assume a Cold War stance by 1947. Or, as simple-minded variations of this theme go, there were all these vacuums in Europe and Asia, and the United States had all this Great Power, and everyone just knows that Great Powers have to use their power.

Recently the focus of this debate has been on the events of 1945, in part because of Alperovitz's detailed analysis of America's "atomic diplomacy" during the middle part of that year, and partly because Arthur Schlesinger Jr. has made the events of Yalta through Potsdam the pivot of his argument in the *Foreign Affairs* article. On perhaps the critical question of this discussion, Louis Halle recently argued the Liberal position in his book, *The Cold War as History:* "The initiative in the Cold War had, from the beginning, been with Moscow."

Halle observed that American policy-makers did not realize as early as they should have that Western and Central Europe formed a near-vacuum inviting the vast Red Army, and Washington officials compounded that error by too rapidly dismantling the American military establishment (a point, incidentally, which Horowitz vigorously disputes, for he believes the Western nations dismantled their armies more slowly than did the Soviets during the 1945–1948 period).

The monopoly of the atomic bomb, Halle continues, meant little, for in the immediate postwar period it was a paper tiger in the sense that it could not be used to correct the balance of power unless the Soviets actually invaded Western Europe.

Horowitz has most directly rejected Halle's thesis: "For the point which I have tried to establish beyond all others, and which has been virtually ignored in previous cold war studies, is that the early post-war power situation was such as to give the United States a near monopoly on the *strategic* decisions which would affect the basic structure of international relations in the post-war period. Conversely, the Kremlin rulers, *whatever their long-range intentions,* were bound by the same imbalance of power to make moves of primarily tactical significance."

In explaining more fully Stalin's responses, revisionists accept an argument first made by Isaac Deutscher. In Oglesby's words: "Stalin's record in the early Cold War is less that of a fairy-tale monster on the prowl . . . than that of a small, cold, very practical nationalist in a tight, dangerous situation. Stalin accepted the Cold War. He seems to have had little choice. . . . But that does not prove that he *created* it. The terms of that eerie battle were mainly set by the power that held the initiative and commanded the heights, and those powers were England in the rear and the United States far out in front."

Oglesby summarizes why the United States was in the vanguard: "The uniformly powerful West wanted—and believed . . . that it had to obtain—a guarantee against the spread of revolution and . . . a guarantee of economic and political access to all of Europe. The unevenly powerful Soviet Union wanted development capital without strings, heavy German machinery, and some reprieve from militant Wagnerism."

Oglesby's words summarize several revisionist assumptions about the origins of the Cold War: the United States was determined to enter a sphere of interest (Eastern Europe) which was Russia's by reason of both historical factors and military occupation; the United States attempted to use its overwhelming power to force Russia's hand in Eastern Europe, thus putting Stalin in a defensive position; and, finally, that in making such an assessment of the situation Stalin was sane and knowledgeable. (One revisionist has suggested that if Liberal historians continue to psychoanalyze Stalin, equal time should be given to Harry Truman, particularly his early insecurity in the White House, his intense jealousy of his presidential powers, and his long-time dislike for the Soviet Union.)

Many revisionists further believe that Roosevelt's death made little difference in postwar American policy, thus disagreeing with some of their colleagues, particularly Alperovitz and Fleming, who argue that basic American policy changed after the advent of Truman. True to their belief in historical continuity, most revisionists believe Truman carried out a policy which went back not only to F.D.R., but to McKinley and the Open Door policies of 1899–1900. . . .

. . . Unlike the revisionists, many of the Liberals are Europe-oriented. These include John Lukacs, Louis Halle, George Kennan, and even Morgenthau and Lippmann who, although they share some revisionist views, sharply diverge in believing that American interests in Asia have small importance. Revisionists place vastly more emphasis on the newly-emerging nations than do the Liberals. The latter see Vietnam in terms of power and on the periphery of American interests, but revisionists see that tragedy as the culmination of American expansion and the requirements which the domestic system imposed upon that expansion.

The revisionist challenge to the standard interpretations of Russian policy, the events of 1945, and the involvement in Asia, however, are only case studies of the broad implications for American historical investigation which the revisionist position holds. The general approaches which the revisionists take in viewing and using history may in the long-run be their most important legacy.

To revisionist minds, for example, Liberals have explained American development by over-compartmentalizing political, economic, social, and intellectual factors, and by placing too little emphasis on the economic. Perhaps because they have never had to concern themselves with fundamental economic issues as did historians during the Progressive and New Deal eras, many present writers seem to assume, consciously or unconsciously, that socio-economic institutions such as the corporation exert only slight influence on the way Americans think and act politically.

Few histories of the Cold War, for example, analyze or even note the fantastic overseas growth of the American corporation since 1950. In Williams' *The Contours of American History,* however, the development of the corporation is used as the unifying theme for nearly the last one-third of the book. Revisionists agree with Dean Acheson, an expert whom the Liberals usually trust, who once observed that these various factors cannot be understood if kept apart in the "intellectual equivalent of a cream separator."

As much as any other students of the American past, these revisionists have tried to restore the concept of a *Weltanschauung,* a world-view, to their history. This represents an attempt to restore a wholeness to a history, and particularly to a diplomatic history, that has become increasingly fragmented both in terms of its analysis of causes and its description of how the policy has been applied in various geographical areas. In examining the American scene as a whole and from the inside out, revisionists are not primarily diplomatic historians, but historians of American history.

They tend to define American foreign policy as the means by which the domestic system is preserved and expanded through its dealings with other states. The reaction of the other states must be taken into account, but the initiative has in the main come from the domestic system.

This is why Horowitz's insistence that the United States has held the dominant power in the post-war world is so crucial; this power has allowed Washington officials to be on the offensive at times and places of their own choosing. If this power has not always resulted in diplomatic victories, the revisionists trace the difficulty not to a lack of power, but beyond the military to the domestic institutions which formulate the policies and only use that power to put the policies into operation. For this reason, the revisionists place special emphasis upon interest groups and decision-making.

In following such paths, the revisionists are under heavy obligation to Charles Beard. His stress on domestic factors influencing foreign policy, his isolation of the economic factor for special consideration, his approach to understanding policy through examination of interest groups, and his belief that history can be used to affect social change have all heavily influenced contemporary revisionists.

They nevertheless differ with him in several interesting respects. With his concentration of broad economic, social, and political currents, Beard never wrote a biographical study and little utilized biographical approaches. When he did so, as in *An Economic Interpretation of the Constitution,* he did it sketchily and narrowly. Present revisionists, on the other hand, fix more on individuals, that place where ideas and institutions meet. This approach becomes especially fruitful when those individuals represent a broad socio-economic class possessing a *Weltanschauung* of its own.

Williams' use of Wilson and Hoover in *The Tragedy,* his use of Shaftesbury in *The Contours,* Gardner's emphasis upon Hull's ideas in *Economic Aspects of New Deal Diplomacy,* and Alperovitz's development of Stimson in *Atomic Diplomacy* come to mind. In this sense, Beard also differed in his belief that the economic interests which led to what he considered unfortunate foreign policy (such as the American entry into World War I) were interests of a few and not a broad spectrum of national interest.

In thus diverging from Beard the revisionists can go farther than the master in demonstrating how policy-makers transfer domestic into foreign policies. Perhaps a major difference between revisionists and the Liberals is that the latter cannot understand how men can act rationally on their perception of the national interest and still have things end so badly. They want policy-makers to change, that is to act more like realists and less like idealists. (Idealists in this context means divorced from reality, hence the realist-idealist false dichotomy so often used in examining American diplomacy.)

Revisionists, however, believe that man can rationally perceive his perception of the nation's domestic interests and his policies still come to a bad lot. Put in the simplest terms, revisionists are willing to ascribe considerably more rationality and clarity to the making of American foreign policy than are the Liberal historians.

Beard, however, particularly the later Beard who is so hotly criticized within the profession for his last books condemning Franklin D. Roosevelt, has strongly influenced the revisionists' fear of power. The results have been manifested in attacks upon Liberal interpretations which eulogize a strong presidency and which laud quick decision–making that requires concentration of power. But beyond this there is a sheer fear of power that Liberal historians do not exhibit, perhaps because the people with whom they tend to agree control that power and have done so for much of the last thirty-five years.

MIDWESTERN FEAR OF POWER

Perhaps also this is due to revisionists having been heavily influenced by a Midwestern brand of populist and progressive thought. Again like Beard, many of the influential revisionists were either reared and/or spent the most formative years of their intellectual development in the Midwest. A key disagreement among revisionists can in part be traced perhaps to their splitting along Eastern-Midwestern lines: those reared in Eastern urban areas where New Deal influences were strong are tenderer toward Roosevelt than those from Midwestern sections where New Dealers were considerably more suspect; the Midwestern historians tend to see little difference between the policies of F.D.R. and Truman.

Revisionists seemingly have a confidence, or at least a hope, in "the people," as Oglesby calls them, that Liberals do not display. Kennan and Halle, for example, condemn public opinion for its influence on policy-making and plead for more control by the professional diplomatic corps to which they belonged. Revisionists will have none of that, asking instead for a decentralization of power.

Williams called for such radical changes in 1965: "The core radical ideals and values of community, equality, democracy, and humaneness simply cannot in the future be realized and sustained—nor should they be sought—through more centralization and consolidation. These radical values can most nearly be realized through decentralization and through the creation of many truly human communities. . . . Such decentralization is technologically and economically possible. Such decentralization is essential if democracy is to be maintained and extended. And such decentralization is psychologically and morally mandatory. Our humanity is being pounded and squeezed out of us by the consolidated power of a nationalist corporate welfare capitalism."

In applauding this statement, Oglesby commented that these remarks were not only "in the grain of American democratic populism," but "also in the grain of the American libertarian right." Oglesby appealed to that "libertarian right" to join the left in this battle. Oglesby's appeal resembles Williams' warning that the left, not having a tradition or power base of its own, must look to such enlightened conservatives as Senator Fulbright, at least "in the short run," if power is to be checked and some order and justice restored to the society and foreign policy.

This appeal for decentralization also appears with considerable variation in the revisionist view of a more perfect foreign policy. They want no part of a Wilsonian community of nations because they believe that this kind of dream leads to wars against nations which refuse to dream that dream. They are therefore quite amenable to spheres-of-interest policies, again in the short run, which the

Cordell Hulls and Dean Rusks of the twentieth century have found so abhorrent. Revisionists hope that these spheres will evolve into nationalistic units and then develop on their own into independent members of a world community. This was in part what Williams meant, perhaps, when he urged American policy-makers to accept an open door for revolution in the newly-emerging nations.

Few revisionists have confidence that sufficient changes will occur in the American society, particularly in the decentralization of power, to ameliorate US foreign policy in the foreseeable future. Most agree with many other historians that consensus rules in American history. It is rather ironic that revisionists share this view with Louis Hartz and Clinton Rossiter and thus have doubted that Staughton Lynd would find a radical tradition in the American past. Revisionists see conflict contained within the consensus. Alternatives are often present and worth exploring, but the consensus triumphs. Unlike the other historians, however, revisionists deplore rather than applaud the consensus, and they search for alternatives to it.

"HISTORY" REPLACES IDEOLOGY

Believing that radical changes are necessary but improbable in the foreseeable future seems a highly frustrating position, but revisionists have sought escape by placing their faith in the study of history, and indeed they tend to view that history through a Judaeo-Christian perspective which is rather uncommon at present among American historians as a whole. A revisionist once commented autobiographically that he easily escaped the ritual but found it considerably more difficult to escape the dogma. An example of this influence: Oglesby's volume, *Containment and Change,* which emerged from a conference at Union Theological Seminary; the books' co-author Richard Schaull, wrote: "For those who are seeking some perspective on history as a basis for their reflection on revolution, the immediate prospects are not encouraging." Marxism and Existentialism, Schaull believed, have been found wanting. The Judaeo-Christian perspective, however, expresses "the conviction that something positive" is "happening in the historical process," to wit "a struggle that is moving forward toward its goal." Schaull then carefully distinguishes this view from the "liberal doctrine of progress."

A faith in history is perhaps the most important and far-reaching of the revisionist views. In one of the most significant articles on American historical writing, Warren Susman commented in a 1964 issue of *American Quarterly* that "in that great era of historical awareness beginning roughly in the 1890s, American intellectuals *did* care. They cared because they realized the vital ideological importance in a society like ours of history and the 'proper' attitudes toward it. They cared because they realized that views held about the past generally had consequences for the present. . . . It was precisely because in our kind of social order history becomes a key to ideology, a key to the world view that shapes programs and actions in the present and future."

This view remained until about 1940, Susman observed, when "a singularly anti-historical spirit" appeared "among the leading figures of our intellectual life. . . . Many of our newer literary vogues— some of them brilliantly evocative of major moral dilemmas of our time to be sure—are deliberately wedded to the present moment alone." In this vein Susman mentioned the works of Nevins and Schlesinger Jr., noting Schlesinger's words that "history is a constant tragedy in which we are all involved, whose keynote is anxiety and frustration, not progress and fulfillment."

Susman commented that in such history written recently "we look in vain for a vision of the past which will enable us to remake the present and the future. Here ideology is specifically rejected. Here we find a history which offers a reinforcement of current moral values and no effective challenge to the decision makers within the social order who do most frequently operate in terms of some view of history, some ideology."

CHALLENGE TO POLICY AND TO HISTORIOGRAPHY

The revisionists are posing fundamental objections to the past quarter-century of American diplomacy, but more generally they are challenging the predominant tendencies of a historiography and the way this historiography has been used to buttress policy. American diplomatic historians have been reluctant to acknowledge the inter-relationship over a long period of time between their history and national policy. When debates on the subject did begin, they too often terminated with the Liberals invoking "scientific" history, and "scientific" research.

It is past time, the revisionists believe, for the admission that for American historians history begins and ends with ideology. Between is the honest and systematic research which both revisionist and Liberal historians can do, should do, and have done. The issue of "scientific" history is no longer interesting. It is simply irrelevant. The problem is not whether the research will be as thorough as possible (that should be assumed), but the questions which the historian will ask when he undertakes his research.

For the foreseeable future it now seems very likely that through-out the American diplomatic history profession such questions will be increasingly revisionist and radical in tone, and will construct a picture of American history that will move so far away from the Liberals that the present revisionists will be revised. One push in this direction is the horror of the Vietnam War and the realization that revisionist history, rather than Liberal history, better ex-plains—and even forecasts—such a tragedy.

Another push is the growing realization that the war, racism, domestic violence, and sundry economic ills pose a fundamental challenge to the whole system, and that revisionists have con-structed the best matrix within which to study that challenge in its entirety.

A third push is the number of diplomatic historians who will receive their PhDs in the 1970s, having matured in a period when the Tragic Sixties, the New Left movements, and the early funda-mental works of revisionists will be accepted as fact and as a logical result rather than as the result of a great aberration.

And finally, this historiography will move into and beyond revi-sionism as present middle-of-the-roaders accept revisionism in many of its parts, thus allowing the present revisionists (who will believe that they have made their points) to become more revisionist in their view of history; this might result both as a reaction to the Liberals' move toward revisionism and the impetus caused by new, young scholars. There seems considerably less likelihood now that there will be a swing against revisionism, as occurred after the revisionists of World War I made their appearance.

Whatever the outcome of the present turmoil among American diplomatic historians, two results are already apparent. First, whether the revisionists are proven wrong, right, or somewhere in-between, the profession has been stirred and the resulting debate is enlivening and broadening the writing of diplomatic history in a manner unmatched since such men as Samuel Flagg Bemis, Thomas A. Bailey, and Julius Pratt built the foundation-stones of the profession—and touched off magnificent controversies of their own. And second, whatever else the revisionists accomplish, perhaps their greatest contribution will be a reaffirmation of the faith that the study of history is the necessary means through which the promise of the past can be transformed into fulfillment. Even if, at times, this requires thinking otherwise.

Suggestions for Further Reading

As indicated in the introduction, the literature on the origins of the cold war is vast and increasing yearly. A complete bibliography would not only require disproportionate space but might also tend to overwhelm and boggle the reader. A detailed bibliography (although already slightly out-of-date) can be found in Walter LaFeber, *America, Russia and the Cold War, 1945–1966* (New York: John Wiley, 1967). Presented here, instead, is a highly selective, yet up-to-date list of works that seem especially crucial to the subject, compiled with the special needs of students in mind. Works used in this volume are not included below.

The early period of Russian-American relations, important as background, is covered in Desmond Donnelly, *Struggle for the World: The Cold War, 1917–1965* (New York: St. Martin, 1965); Thomas A. Bailey, *America Faces Russia* (Ithaca: Cornell University Press, 1950); Andre Fontaine, *History of the Cold War from the October Revolution to the Korean War, 1917–1950* (New York: Pantheon Books, 1968); and, from the revisionist standpoint, William A. Williams, *American-Russian Relations, 1781–1947* (New York: Holt, Rinehart & Winston, 1952). More detailed examination of crucial episodes in the pre–1941 period can be found in G. F. Kennan, *Soviet-American Relations, 1917–1920,* 2 Vols. [Vol. 1. *Russia Leaves the War;* Vol. 2. *The Decision to Intervene.*] (Princeton: Princeton University Press, 1956, 1958); Betty Unterberger, ed., *American Intervention in the Russian Civil War* (Lexington, Mass.: D. C. Heath, 1969); Peter G. Filene, *Americans and the Soviet Experiment 1917–1933* (Cambridge, Mass.: Harvard University Press, 1967); Robert Browder, *The Origins of Soviet-American Diplomacy* (Princeton: Princeton University Press, 1953); and Edward Bennett, *Recognition of Russia: An American Foreign Policy Dilemma* (Waltham, Mass.: Ginn, 1970).

The diplomacy of the Second World War is obviously essential to any understanding of what happened afterwards. Brief summaries can be found in Gaddis Smith, *American Diplomacy During the*

Second World War, 1941–1945 (New York: John Wiley, 1965); John L. Snell, *Illusion and Necessity: The Diplomacy of Global War* (Boston: Houghton Mifflin, 1963); Robert Divine, *Second Chance: The Triumph of Internationalism in America During World War II* (New York: Atheneum, 1967); and *Roosevelt and World War II* (Baltimore: Johns Hopkins Press, 1969). More detailed accounts are found in the standard works by Herbert Feis, *Churchill, Roosevelt and Stalin: The War They Waged and the Peace They Sought* (Princeton: Princeton University Press, 1957); *Between War and Peace: The Potsdam Conference* (Princeton: Princeton University Press, 1960); and in William H. McNeill, *America, Britain and Russia: Their Cooperation and Conflict, 1941–1946* (New York: Johnson Reprint, 1953). The latter work, less well known than it deserves to be, contains some remarkable insights for a book published while the cold war in its classic form still raged.

There are no works covering the first two post-war years as such. Students should consult the appropriate chapters in the general histories of the cold war, of post-war international relations, and of American foreign policy. The most satisfactory account is Walter LaFeber, *America, Russia and the Cold War, 1945–1966* (New York: John Wiley, 1967). A briefer account can be found in Norman Graebner, *Cold War Diplomacy: American Foreign Policy, 1945–1960* (Princeton: Van Nostrand-Reinhold, 1962). More traditional views are represented by G. F. Hudson, *The Hard and Bitter Peace: World Politics Since 1945* (New York: Praeger, 1967); Paul Y. Hammond, *The Cold War Years: American Foreign Policy Since 1945* (New York: Harcourt Brace Jovanovitch, 1969); Herbert Druks, *Harry S. Truman and the Russians, 1945–1953* (New York: Speller, 1966); Dexter Perkins, *The Diplomacy of a New Age: Major Issues in U.S. Policy Since 1945* (Bloomington: Indiana University Press, 1967); Paul Seabury, *The Rise and Fall of the Cold War* (New York: Basic Books, 1967); Seyom Brown, *The Faces of Power: Constancy & Change in U.S. Foreign Policy from Truman to Johnson* (New York: Columbia University Press, 1968); W. W. Rostow, *The United States in the World Arena* (New York: Harper & Row, 1960); G. F. Kennan, *Russia and the West Under Lenin and Stalin* (Boston: Little, Brown, 1959); and John Lukacs, *A New*

History of the Cold War (Garden City: Anchor, 1966). Although all of these works can be considered of the orthodox school, some are critical of aspects of American policy for being exaggerated or lacking in "realism": Kennan, Seabury and, to a lesser extent, Perkins and Lukacs fall into this category.

General works representing in varying degrees the revisionist dissent include Ronald Steel, *Pax Americana* (New York: Viking, 1967); N. D. Houghton, ed., *Struggle Against History: U.S. Foreign Policy in an Age of Revolution* (New York: Simon & Schuster, 1968); Thomas Paterson, ed., *Cold War Critics: Alternatives to American Foreign Policy in the Truman Administration* (Chicago: Quadrangle Books, 1970); Richard Barnet and Marcus Raskin, *After Twenty Years: Alternatives to the Cold War in Europe* (New York: Random House, 1965); David Horowitz, ed., *Containment and Revolution* (Boston: Beacon Press, 1967); Frederick Schuman, *The Cold War: Retrospect and Prospect* (Baton Rouge: Louisiana State University Press, 1967); and Carl Oglesby and Richard Schaull, *Containment and Change: Two Dissenting Views of American Society and Foreign Policy in the New Revolutionary Age* (New York: Macmillan, 1967).

Other general works of interest include William L. Neumann, *After Victory* (New York: Harper & Row, 1967); William Carleton, *The Revolution in American Foreign Policy* (New York: Random House, 1967); Robert Osgood, *et al., America and the World: From the Truman Doctrine to Vietnam* (Baltimore: Johns Hopkins University Press, 1970); Robert Warth, *Soviet Russia in World Politics* (New York: Twayne, 1963); and J. M. Mackintosh, *Strategy and Tactics of Soviet Foreign Policy* (London: Oxford University Press, 1962).

On the specific areas of cold war tension treated in this book there are many specialized studies. On the atomic bomb and disarmament problems: Herbert Feis, *The Atomic Bomb and the End of World War II* (Princeton: Princeton University Press, 1966) accepts the conventional justification for the use of the bomb, while P. M. S. Blackett, *Fear, War and the Bomb* (New York: McGraw-Hill, 1948) is an early harbinger of the Alperovitz thesis. Bernard Bechhoefer,

Post War Negotiations for Arms Control (Washington: Burns & MacEachern, 1961) and John Spanier and Joseph Nogee, *The Politics of Disarmament: A Study in Soviet-American Gamesmanship:* (New York: Praeger, 1962) deal with attempts at control after the war. See also David E. Lilienthal, *Journals: Atomic Energy Years, 1945–1950* (New York: Harper & Row, 1964).

On American economic policy (including the Russian loan) see Lloyd Gardner, *Economic Aspects of New Deal Diplomacy* (Madison: University of Wisconsin Press, 1964); Richard Gardner, *Sterling-Dollar Diplomacy* (New York: McGraw-Hill, 1969); and E. F. Penrose, *Economic Planning for Peace* (Princeton: Princeton University Press, 1953).

On Germany and Eastern Europe see John Gimbel, *The American Occupation of Germany: Politics and the Military, 1945–1949* (Stanford: Stanford University Press, 1968); Manuel Gottlieb, *The German Peace Settlement and the Berlin Crisis* (New York: Paine-Whitman, 1960); J. P. Nettl, *The Eastern Zone and Soviet Policy in Germany, 1945–1950* (London: Oxford, 1951); Hugh Seton-Watson, *The East European Revolution* (New York: Praeger, 1956); Stephen Kertesz, ed., *The Fate of East Central Europe* (Notre Dame, Ind.; University of Notre Dame Press, 1956). See also the memoir of American Ambassador Arthur Bliss Lane, *I Saw Poland Betrayed* (Indianapolis: Bobbs-Merrill, 1948).

On the Truman Doctrine and the containment policy: Stephen Xydis, *Greece and the Great Powers, 1944–1947* (Chicago: Argonaut, 1963); and Joseph M. Jones, *Fifteen Weeks* (New York: Harcourt Brace Jovanovitch, 1955). The latter book provides an almost hour-by-hour account of the events leading up to the Truman message to Congress. Walter Lippmann, *The Cold War: A Study in American Foreign Policy* (New York: Harper & Row, 1947) is a trenchant contemporary critique of containment along lines to be followed later by revisionist historians.

Although confined to Europe, cold war problems in other areas which were to become formidable later, have been interpreted by

Tsang Tsou, *America's Failure in China, 1941-1950* (Chicago: University of Chicago Press, 1963); Herbert Feis, *Contest Over Japan: The Soviet Bid for Power in the Far East* (New York: W. W. Norton, 1967); George Kahin and John Lewis, *The United States in Vietnam* (New York: Dial Press, 1967); George Kirk, *The Middle East* (London: Royal Institute of International Affairs, 1954); and J. Lloyd Mecham, *A Survey of United States-Latin American Relations* (Boston: Houghton Mifflin, 1965).

Key figures in the origins of the cold war can be studied in memoirs and secondary sources. Fundamental, of course, is Harry S. Truman, *Years of Decisions* and *Years of Trial and Hope* (New York: Doubleday, 1955, 1956). Also useful are James F. Byrnes, *Speaking Frankly* (New York: Harper & Row, 1947); Dean G. Acheson, *Present at the Creation: My Years in the State Department* (New York: W. W. Norton, 1969); William Leahy, *I Was There* (New York: McGraw-Hill, 1950); Walter Bedell Smith, *My Three Years in Moscow* (Philadelphia: J. B. Lippincott, 1950); and Henry L. Stimson and McGeorge Bundy, *On Active Service in Peace and War* (New York: Harper & Row, 1948). G. F. Kennan, *Memoirs 1925-1950* (Boston: Little, Brown, 1967) is of special interest and Walter Millis, ed., *The Forrestal Diaries* (New York: Viking Press, 1951) should also be consulted. The secretaries of state in the years 1943-1947 are concisely treated in N. A. Graebner, ed., *An Uncertain Tradition: American Secretaries of State in the Twentieth Century* (New York: McGraw-Hill, 1961), and more extensively covered in Robert Ferrell, ed., *American Secretaries of State and their Diplomacy,* Vols. 13, 14, 15 (New York: Cooper Square, 1964, 1965). Cabell Phillips, *The Truman Presidency* (New York: Penguin Books, 1966) and Jonathan Daniels, *The Man of Independence* (Philadelphia: J. B. Lippincott, 1950) should be balanced by Barton Bernstein and Allen Matusow, *The Truman Administration: A Documentary History* (New York: Harper & Row, 1966). Isaac Deutscher's *Stalin: A Political Biography* (New York: Oxford University Press, 1966) is an arresting interpretation.

The historiographic controversy can be traced in Christopher Lasch, "The Cold War Revisited and Revisioned," *New York Times*

Magazine (January 14, 1968); H. Stuart Hughes, "The Second Year of the Cold War: A Memoir and an Anticipation," *Commentary*, XLVIII (August, 1969); Norman A. Graebner, "Cold War Origins and the Contemporary Debate," *Journal of Conflict Resolution*, XIII (March, 1969); Staughton Lynd, "How the Cold War Began," *Commentary*, XXX (November, 1960); John Snell, "The Cold War: Four Contemporary Appraisals," *American Historical Review*, LXVIII (October, 1962); Gar Alperovitz, "How Did the Cold War Begin?," *New York Review of Books* (March 23, 1967); Paul Seabury and Brian Thomas, "Cold War Origins," *Journal of Contemporary History*, III (January, 1968); Henry Pachter, "Revisionist Historians and the Cold War," *Dissent* (November, 1968).

Finally, documentation on cold war origins can be found in the appropriate volumes of the Department of State's *Foreign Relations of the United States* and the *Department of State Bulletin*, the Council on Foreign Relations' *Documents of American Foreign Relations* and The Royal Institute of International Affairs' *Documents on International Affairs*. Other than the Soviet Foreign Ministry's fairly brief *Correspondence Between the Chairman of the Council of Ministers of the USSR and the Presidents of the USA and the Prime Ministers of Great Britain During the Great Patriotic War of 1941–1945* (Moscow, 1957), the Moscow archives remain sealed to western eyes.